Ancient Civilizations
A Journey Through Time

by

Anup Singh

Double9 BOOKS

Ancient Civilizations

A Journey Through Time

by Anup Singh

ISBN: 978-93-67141-58-8

Published by

DOUBLE 9 BOOKS

2/13-B, Ansari Road
Daryaganj, New Delhi – 110002
info@double9books.com
www.double9books.com
Tel. 011-40042856

ABOUT THE AUTHOR

Anup Singh is a class 8th Student, and this is going to be his 2nd published book. His first book "Bhakti an Religious" was a successful book. Anup Singh had a very good knowledge of History. He is a certified Prompt Engineer from Be10X. He is a certified author from Som Bhatla Author's Academy and Double 9 Books, and he had also cracked the exam of National Author's Academy batch 2021-22 & 2023-24. Anup Singh has also represented his School & Block at District Level Quiz Competition. Anup Singh had also a very good knowledge of Author's and their Books. Recently, in the month of March,2024 Anup Singh had cracked National Scholarship Test for Young Author's (NSTYA) with All India Rank 4 (AIR 4).

CONTENTS

Preface

Studying ancient civilizations is like embarking on a time- travel adventure through the pages of history. These civilizations, some of the earliest and most influential societies in human history, laid the foundations for many aspects of our modern world. From governance systems and legal codes to architectural marvels and philosophical ideas, their contributions continue to shape our lives today. This book aims to provide a comprehensive and engaging exploration of several key ancient civilizations: Egypt, Greece, Rome, the Indus Valley, Persia, Mesopotamia, China, and Japan.

Understanding ancient civilizations not only broadens your knowledge of the past but also enhances your appreciation for the cultural and technological advancements that define our present. Each chapter in this book is carefully structured to give you a well-rounded view of these ancient societies, focusing on their geography, society, culture, achievements, and religious beliefs.

The journey begins with Ancient Egypt, the land of the pharaohs, where the mighty Nile River nurtured a civilization renowned for its pyramids, hieroglyphics, and profound religious beliefs. From there, we will travel to Ancient Greece, the cradle of Western philosophy, democracy, and the Olympic Games. Next, we will explore the grandeur of Ancient Rome, whose legal and political systems have left an indelible mark on modern governance. The Indus Valley Civilization, with its advanced urban planning and mysterious script, will be our next stop, offering insights into one of the earliest urban cultures.

In the chapters that follow, we will delve into the vast and culturally rich Persian Empire, whose administrative prowess and religious innovations played a significant role in shaping ancient history. Ancient Mesopotamia, often called the "Cradle of Civilization," will reveal the origins of writing, legal systems, and urban development. Ancient China, with its enduring dynasties and profound philosophical traditions, will illustrate the complexity and continuity of Chinese culture. Finally, Ancient Japan will introduce us to the unique blend of Shintoism and Buddhism that has shaped Japanese identity and cultural heritage.

This book is designed not just to inform but also to inspire. Each chapter includes stories of remarkable individuals, significant events, and groundbreaking inventions that highlight the ingenuity and resilience of these ancient peoples. By studying their achievements and learning from their challenges, we can gain valuable lessons that are relevant even in our modern world.

To make this book as engaging as possible, we have included a variety of illustrations, maps, and timelines to help visualize the information. Key terms and concepts are explained in simple language, and each chapter ends with a summary and questions to encourage further reflection and discussion.

The exploration of ancient civilizations is not just about memorizing dates and facts; it is about connecting with the human stories that have shaped our world. It is about understanding the diversity of human experience and recognizing the common threads that unite us across time and space. We hope this book will ignite your curiosity and foster a lifelong interest in history and culture.

Thank you for embarking on this journey with us. Let the adventure begin!

-Anup Singh

Introduction

The study of ancient civilizations provides a window into the distant past, offering a glimpse of how early human societies developed, thrived, and interacted with their environments and each other. By examining the histories of civilizations such as Egypt, Greece, Rome, the Indus Valley, Persia, Mesopotamia, China, and Japan, we can uncover the roots of many contemporary practices, institutions, and ideas.

The Importance of Studying Ancient Civilizations

Understanding ancient civilizations is crucial for several reasons. Firstly, it helps us comprehend the origins of modern society. Many foundational aspects of our current world—such as writing systems, legal frameworks, architectural techniques, and religious beliefs—can be traced back to these early societies. Secondly, studying ancient civilizations allows us to appreciate the diversity and ingenuity of human cultures. Each civilization developed unique solutions to the challenges of their time, reflecting the creativity and resilience of their people. Lastly, exploring ancient history can inspire us to think critically about our own society. By learning about the successes and failures of the past, we can gain insights into how to address contemporary issues and build a better future.

The Interconnectedness of Ancient Civilizations

Although these ancient civilizations developed independently, they were not isolated. Trade routes, wars, migrations, and cultural exchanges linked them together, fostering a flow of ideas, goods, and technologies. The Silk Road, for example, connected the East and West, allowing for the exchange of silk, spices, ideas, and even diseases. This interconnectedness is a reminder that human societies have always been part of a global network, influencing and being influenced by one another.

Themes to Explore in Ancient Civilizations

Several recurring themes can be observed across these ancient civilizations, offering valuable insights into the human condition and the development of societies.

1. **Governance and Political Systems:**

    - Ancient civilizations experimented with various forms of governance, from the pharaohs of Egypt and the emperors of China to the democratic practices of Athens and the republic of Rome. Understanding these systems helps us see the origins of modern political thought and governance.

2. **Religion and Mythology:**

    - Religion played a central role in shaping the values, behaviours, and cultures of ancient civilizations. From the polytheistic beliefs of Mesopotamia and Egypt to the philosophical traditions of China and the monotheistic Zoroastrianism of Persia, religious and mythological stories provided explanations for natural phenomena, moral guidance, and a sense of purpose.

3. **Social Structure and Daily Life:**

    - Social hierarchies and roles were clearly defined in ancient societies. The division of labour, class distinctions, and family structures influenced daily life and social interactions. Examining these aspects reveals the organization of labour, gender roles, and the distribution of wealth and power.

4. **Science, Technology, and Innovation:**

    - Ancient civilizations were centres of innovation, contributing to fields such as mathematics, astronomy, engineering, and medicine. The achievements of these early societies laid the groundwork for modern science and technology.

5. **Art, Literature, and Culture:**

    - Artistic expressions, literature, and cultural practices provide a window into the values and beliefs of ancient peoples. From the epic poems of Homer to the intricate pottery of the Indus Valley, these cultural artifacts continue to inspire and inform us.

6. Economics and Trade:

- Trade and economic practices were vital for the survival and growth of ancient civilizations. The exchange of goods, services, and ideas facilitated cultural diffusion and economic prosperity. Understanding these economic systems offers lessons in resource management and economic integration.

Challenges and Declines

Despite their achievements, ancient civilizations also faced significant challenges that led to their decline. Environmental changes, resource depletion, internal strife, and external invasions were common factors that contributed to the fall of these once-great societies. Studying these challenges helps us understand the fragility of civilizations and the importance of sustainable practices and effective governance.

Learning from the Past

The study of ancient civilizations is not just an academic exercise; it has practical implications for our contemporary world. By learning about the successes and failures of the past, we can draw lessons that are relevant today. For instance, the collapse of the Roman Empire due to overexpansion and political corruption serves as a cautionary tale about the limits of power and the need for sound governance. Similarly, the environmental practices of ancient societies offer insights into sustainable living and the consequences of resource mismanagement.

How to Use This Book

This book is designed to be accessible and engaging for Class 8 students. Each chapter focuses on a specific civilization, providing an overview of its geography, society, culture, achievements, and religion. The chapters are structured to highlight key themes and concepts, making it easier to understand and remember the information. Additionally, the book includes:

- **Illustrations and Maps:** Visual aids to help you visualize the locations, structures, and artifacts of each civilization.
- **Timelines:** Chronological timelines to contextualize major events and developments.
- **Summaries and Key Terms:** End-of-chapter summaries and definitions of important terms to reinforce learning.

- **Questions and Activities:** Questions and activities designed to encourage critical thinking and further exploration of the topics.

Conclusion

Embarking on the study of ancient civilizations is like opening a door to a world of wonder and wisdom. As you read through the chapters, you'll encounter the ingenuity and resilience of our ancestors, their triumphs and tribulations, and the rich tapestry of human history. This exploration will not only enhance your understanding of the past but also inspire you to think critically about the present and the future. Let this book be your guide as you journey through time, discovering the legacy of ancient civilizations and the enduring impact they have on our world today.

Chapter 1
Introduction to Ancient Civilizations

Ancient civilizations stand as the foundation upon which our modern societies have been built. They are the cradles of human innovation, culture, and societal organization, providing us with a window into our collective past and shaping the course of human history. In this chapter, we will delve into the definition and characteristics of ancient civilizations, explore the importance of studying them, and provide a brief overview of eight major civilizations: Egypt, Greece, Rome, Indus Valley, Persia, Mesopotamia, China and Japan.

What is an Ancient Civilization?

Ancient civilizations are complex societies that emerged thousands of years ago and were characterized by various defining features. One key characteristic is the development of sophisticated urban centers, where large populations resided and engaged in various economic, political, and cultural activities. These cities often served as hubs of trade, administration, and religious practices.

Another hallmark of ancient civilizations is the presence of advanced social hierarchies. These societies were typically stratified, with distinct social classes such as rulers, priests, artisans, merchants, and peasants. The division of labor and social roles was often rigidly defined, contributing to the stability and functionality of these civilizations.

Furthermore, ancient civilizations exhibited remarkable advancements in technology, agriculture, architecture, and the arts. They developed writing systems to record information, created monumental structures such as temples and palaces, and produced intricate artwork and literature that reflected their beliefs, values, and aspirations.

Importance of Studying Ancient Civilizations

Studying ancient civilizations is crucial for several reasons. Firstly, it provides us with insights into the origins of human societies and the processes of cultural development and evolution. By examining how ancient civilizations organized themselves, interacted with their environment, and addressed challenges, we can gain a deeper understanding of our own cultural heritage and societal structures.

Moreover, the study of ancient civilizations helps us appreciate the diversity of human experiences and perspectives throughout history. Each civilization had its unique customs, beliefs, and achievements, contributing to the rich tapestry of human civilization. By exploring these diverse narratives, we can cultivate empathy, tolerance, and appreciation for cultural differences.

Additionally, studying ancient civilizations allows us to learn valuable lessons that are relevant to contemporary issues and challenges. Many of the issues faced by ancient societies, such as resource management, political instability, and social inequality, continue to resonate in our world today. By analysing how ancient civilizations grappled with these issues, we can glean insights that inform our own efforts to build more sustainable, equitable, and resilient societies.

Overview of Major Civilizations

Egypt:

Ancient Egypt is one of the most iconic civilizations in history, known for its monumental architecture, intricate hieroglyphic writing, and rich religious traditions. Cantered along the fertile banks of the Nile River, Egyptian civilization flourished for over three millennia, from around 3100 BCE to 30 BCE. The ancient Egyptians developed sophisticated irrigation systems, built monumental pyramids and temples, and created a complex pantheon of gods and goddesses. Their contributions to mathematics, medicine, and astronomy laid the groundwork for future scientific advancements.

Greece:

Ancient Greece is renowned for its contributions to philosophy, democracy, and the arts. From the Mycenaean and Minoan civilizations to the classical period of Athens and Sparta, Greek civilization spanned over a thousand years, from around 2700 BCE to 146 BCE. The Greeks made significant advances in fields such as mathematics, literature, and theatre, and their cultural legacy continues to influence Western thought and civilization to this day.

Rome:

Ancient Rome is often regarded as one of the most influential civilizations in history, known for its vast empire, sophisticated infrastructure, and legal system. Founded in the 8th century BCE, Rome grew from a small city-state to a mighty empire that encompassed much of Europe, North Africa, and the Middle East. The Romans excelled in engineering, architecture, and military strategy, leaving behind enduring monuments such as the Colosseum and the aqueducts. Their legacy also includes contributions to governance, law, and language, as evidenced by the enduring influence of Latin and Roman legal principles.

Indus Valley:

The Indus Valley civilization, also known as the Harappan civilization, emerged around 3300 BCE in the fertile plains of the Indus River valley in present-day Pakistan and northwest India. It was one of the world's earliest urban civilizations, with well-planned cities, advanced sanitation systems, and a thriving trade network that extended across the region. Although much about the Indus Valley civilization remains enigmatic due to the lack of decipherable written records, archaeological evidence suggests a sophisticated society with a high level of technological and cultural achievement.

In conclusion, ancient civilizations represent the collective achievements and legacies of our ancestors. By studying these civilizations, we gain valuable insights into the complexities of human societies, the diversity of human cultures, and the enduring quest for knowledge and innovation. Egypt, Greece, Rome, and the Indus Valley are just a few examples of the rich tapestry of ancient civilizations that have shaped our world and continue to inspire us today.

Persian:

The Persian Empire, under the leadership of Cyrus the Great and his successors, became one of the most powerful empires of the ancient world. It was characterized by its tolerance of diverse cultures and religions within its vast territories, which extended from the Indus Valley to Greece and Egypt. The Persians developed an efficient administrative system with satraps (provincial governors) overseeing different regions. They also made significant contributions to infrastructure, including the construction of the Royal Road and the use of an early postal system. Zoroastrianism, the main religion of Persia, had a profound influence on later religious traditions.

Mesopotamia:

Mesopotamia, often referred to as the "Cradle of Civilization," was home to some of the earliest known cities and empires, including Sumer, Akkad, Babylon, and Assyria. Located between the Tigris and Euphrates rivers,

Mesopotamia saw the development of cuneiform writing, one of the earliest writing systems. The Code of Hammurabi, a comprehensive set of laws from Babylon, represents one of the earliest examples of written law. Mesopotamian society was highly stratified, and its contributions to mathematics, astronomy, and literature, such as the Epic of Gilgamesh, are still studied today.

China:

China, with its enduring dynasties and profound philosophical traditions, developed in the fertile valleys of the Yellow and Yangtze Rivers. The early dynasties, such as the Shang and Zhou, laid the foundations for Chinese civilization. The Qin Dynasty, although short-lived, unified China and standardized many aspects of society, including weights, measures, and the written script. The Han Dynasty followed, ushering in a golden age of cultural and scientific achievements. Confucianism and Daoism, two major philosophical systems, emerged during this period and deeply influenced Chinese society and governance.

Japan:

Japan developed in relative isolation, leading to a unique blend of cultural and religious practices. Early Japanese society was organized into clans, with the Yamato clan eventually establishing dominance and laying the foundation for the imperial system. Shintoism, the indigenous religion, played a central role in Japanese culture, emphasizing the worship of kami (spirits) and the importance of ritual purity. Buddhism, introduced from China and Korea, also became influential, leading to a syncretism of religious beliefs. Japanese society developed distinctive art forms, literature, and a strong warrior tradition exemplified by the samurai.

Chapter 2
Ancient Egypt

Ancient Egypt stands as a testament to human ingenuity, resilience, and cultural achievement. From the fertile banks of the Nile emerged a civilization that flourished for millennia, leaving behind a legacy of monumental architecture, artistic mastery, and enduring spiritual beliefs. Despite the passage of millennia, the legacy of Ancient Egypt continues to captivate and inspire, serving as a reminder of the timeless allure of human creativity and ambition.

Geography and Early Settlement

Nestled along the fertile banks of the Nile River, Ancient Egypt emerged as one of the world's most remarkable civilizations. The Nile, with its annual inundation, served as the lifeblood of Egyptian society, shaping its economy, culture, and religious beliefs. Flowing south to north, the Nile provided a consistent water source for agriculture and facilitated trade and communication between Upper and Lower Egypt.

The significance of the Nile cannot be overstated. Its predictable floodwaters deposited nutrient-rich silt onto the riverbanks, creating fertile land conducive to agriculture. Egyptians developed sophisticated irrigation systems to harness the Nile's waters, enabling the cultivation of crops such as wheat, barley, and flax. The abundance of food provided by the Nile allowed Egyptian society to flourish, supporting a population that engaged in various economic activities, including farming, fishing, and trade.

Society and Culture

Ancient Egyptian society was characterized by a hierarchical structure that reflected both social status and religious beliefs. At the pinnacle of the social hierarchy was the pharaoh, who was not only the political ruler but also considered a divine figure, embodying the gods on Earth. Beneath the pharaoh were priests, scribes, artisans, and peasants, each playing essential roles in maintaining the stability and prosperity of Egyptian civilization.

Priests served as intermediaries between the people and the gods, overseeing religious rituals and ceremonies that were central to Egyptian life. Scribes, highly esteemed for their literacy and administrative skills, were responsible for recording information, maintaining official documents, and managing the affairs of the state. Artisans and craftsmen demonstrated remarkable skill in various trades, producing exquisite works of art, jewellery, and pottery that adorned both temples and tombs.

Peasants formed the backbone of Egyptian society, toiling in the fields to ensure a steady food supply and contributing labour to monumental construction projects such as the pyramids. Despite their vital role, peasants held lower social status and often lived modestly, residing in simple mud-brick houses, and relying on subsistence farming for survival.

Daily life in ancient Egypt was governed by tradition, ritual, and the cyclical rhythms of the Nile. Egyptians typically wore lightweight linen garments suited to the hot climate, with men wearing kilts and women donning ankle-length dresses. A staple of the Egyptian diet was bread, made from emmer wheat and barley, supplemented by vegetables, fruits, and fish from the Nile. Beer, brewed from barley, was a common beverage, while wine was reserved for special occasions.

Achievements and Contributions

Ancient Egypt left an indelible mark on history through its monumental architecture, technological innovations, and cultural achievements. Perhaps most iconic are the pyramids, massive stone structures built as royal tombs to ensure the pharaoh's eternal life in the after worlds. The Great Pyramid of Giza, constructed during the reign of Pharaoh Khufu in the 26th century BCE, stands as a testament to the ingenuity and engineering prowess of the ancient Egyptians.

Hieroglyphics, the ancient Egyptian writing system, played a crucial role in recording history, religion, and administration. Comprising thousands of pictorial symbols, hieroglyphics adorned temple walls, royal monuments, and papyrus scrolls. The discovery of the Rosetta Stone in 1799 proved instrumental in deciphering hieroglyphics, providing scholars with a key to unlock the mysteries of ancient Egyptian civilization.

In addition to their architectural and linguistic achievements, the ancient Egyptians made significant contributions to fields such as medicine and mathematics. Egyptian physicians developed a sophisticated understanding of anatomy and medical treatments, including surgical procedures, herbal remedies, and the use of medical instruments. Mathematical knowledge was applied in various practical contexts, such as surveying land for agricultural purposes and calculating the dimensions of pyramids and other structures.

Religion and Mythology

Religion permeated every aspect of ancient Egyptian life, shaping beliefs about the cosmos, the afterlife, and the divine order of the universe. The Egyptian pantheon comprised a vast array of gods and goddesses, each associated with specific aspects of nature, fertility, and human affairs. Among the most prominent deities were Ra, the sun god; Osiris, the god of the afterlife; Isis, the goddess of magic and motherhood; and Hathor, the goddess of love and music.

Central to Egyptian religious beliefs was the concept of ma 'at, representing cosmic order, justice, and truth. Egyptians believed that maintaining ma 'at was essential for harmony in both the earthly realm and the afterlife. To ensure a prosperous journey to the afterlife, individuals underwent the process of mummification, in which the body was preserved through a meticulous embalming process and placed in a tomb along with provisions and funerary goods. The Egyptian pantheon comprised a multitude of gods and goddesses, each with their own distinct attributes, responsibilities, and mythological narratives. Ra, the sun god, was among the most revered deities, symbolizing the life-giving power of the sun and the cycles of creation and renewal. Ra was often depicted as a falcon-headed figure, sailing across the sky in his solar barque during the day and journeying through the underworld at night.

Osiris, the god of the afterlife and resurrection, played a central role in Egyptian mythology. He was believed to be the ruler of the underworld, where he presided over the judgment of souls and granted eternal life to the virtuous. Osiris was frequently depicted as a mummified figure, symbolizing the cycle of death and rebirth, and his myth served as a source of hope and comfort for the deceased and their loved ones.

Isis, the goddess of magic and motherhood, was revered as a powerful protector and healer. She was the sister and wife of Osiris, and together they represented the divine principles of fertility, nurturing, and renewal. Isis was often depicted with outstretched wings, embracing the deceased in a gesture of compassion and protection, and her cult spread throughout Egypt and beyond, enduring for millennia.

Hathor, the goddess of love, music, and joy, embodied the pleasures and delights of life. She was often depicted as a cow goddess or as a woman with the ears of a cow, symbolizing fertility and maternal nurturing. Hathor was associated with music, dance, and festivities, and her presence was believed to bring happiness, abundance, and prosperity to the people of Egypt.

Beliefs about the Afterlife and Mummification:

Central to Egyptian religious beliefs was the concept of the afterlife, a realm of eternal existence beyond the physical world. Egyptians believed that life continued after death, and that the deceased embarked on a perilous journey to reach the realm of the gods and achieve immortality. To ensure a successful transition to the afterlife, individuals underwent the process of mummification, a complex and highly ritualized practice that preserved the body for eternity.

Mummification involved several stages, beginning with the removal of internal organs and their preservation in jars known as canopic jars. The body was then cleaned and dried before being wrapped in linen bandages, with amulets and charms placed among the wrappings to provide protection and magical assistance in the afterlife. Finally, the mummy was placed in a coffin or sarcophagus adorned with religious inscriptions and symbols, ready to journey to the realm of the gods.

The elaborate rituals surrounding mummification reflected the Egyptians' profound reverence for the dead and their belief in the continuity of life beyond the grave. The preservation of the body was essential to ensure that the deceased could recognize and inhabit their physical form in the afterlife, where they would be reunited with their loved ones and enjoy eternal bliss in the presence of the gods.

In conclusion, the religion and mythology of ancient Egypt provided a rich tapestry of beliefs and rituals that guided every aspect of Egyptian life, from birth to death and beyond. The pantheon of gods and goddesses, with their diverse attributes and mythological narratives, offered comfort, guidance, and meaning to the people of Egypt, shaping their worldview and cultural identity for millennia. Despite the passage of time, the legacy of Egyptian religion continues to captivate and inspire, serving as a testament to the enduring power of human spirituality and imagination.

Chapter 3
Ancient Greece

Ancient Greece, a civilization shaped by its geography and rich in cultural achievements, profoundly influenced Western civilization. From the contrasting city-states of Athens and Sparta to groundbreaking contributions in philosophy, science, and the arts, Greece's legacy endures. This chapter explores the geography, society, achievements, and mythology of ancient Greece.

Geography and City-States

Ancient Greece was a civilization profoundly shaped by its geography, with the Mediterranean Sea playing a crucial role in its development. The Greeks inhabited a mountainous peninsula and numerous islands, which fostered the growth of independent city-states, each with its own distinct culture and political system. The rugged terrain made large-scale farming difficult but encouraged seafaring, trade, and colonization.

The Significance of the Mediterranean Sea

The Mediterranean Sea was the lifeblood of ancient Greece, influencing its economy, culture, and interactions with neighbouring civilizations. The Greeks became adept sailors and traders, establishing colonies and trade networks across the Mediterranean and Black Seas. This connectivity facilitated the exchange of goods, ideas, and cultural practices, contributing to the rich tapestry of Greek civilization.

The sea provided abundant resources, including fish, which was a staple of the Greek diet. It also offered a means of transport and communication, crucial for the fragmented Greek world. The Greek ships, known for their speed and manoeuvrability, enabled the establishment of trade routes that linked Greece with Egypt, Phoenicia, and other Mediterranean cultures, allowing for the import of grains, metals, and luxury goods.

Differences between Athens and Sparta

Among the numerous Greek city-states, Athens and Sparta were the most prominent, each representing contrasting societal models and values.

Athens

Athens is renowned for its development of democracy and its cultural achievements. In the 5th century BCE, Athens established a direct democracy where citizens participated in decision-making processes. The Athenian Assembly, open to all male citizens, played a crucial role in governance, debating and voting on laws and policies. This system of governance fostered a sense of civic duty and involvement among the Athenians.

Athenian society was also distinguished by its emphasis on education, philosophy, and the arts. Education was highly valued, with a focus on literature, rhetoric, and physical training. The city became a hub for intellectual and artistic activity, producing some of the greatest philosophers, playwrights, and artists of the ancient world.

Sparta

In stark contrast, Sparta was a militaristic society known for its rigorous training and discipline. The Spartan system focused on creating a formidable warrior class. From a young age, boys underwent the agoge, a state-sponsored education and training program designed to instil physical prowess, endurance, and loyalty to the state. Spartan society was highly regimented, with an emphasis on austerity, self-discipline, and communal living.

While Sparta's political structure included elements of oligarchy and monarchy, it was the military that dominated all aspects of life. The ruling class, known as the Spartiate's, held full political rights, while the larger population of helots, or state-owned serfs, performed agricultural labour to sustain the economy. This rigid social structure ensured the Spartans' focus remained on military excellence and state security.

Society and Culture

Democracy in Athens

The Athenian democracy was revolutionary for its time, emphasizing the role of citizens in governance. The system included institutions such as the Assembly (Ekklesia), the Council of 500 (Boule), and various courts. The Assembly was the main legislative body where citizens could propose and debate laws. The Council of 500, chosen by lot from the citizens, handled daily administrative tasks and prepared issues for discussion in the Assembly. Additionally, various courts, staffed by large juries of citizens, adjudicated legal disputes.

This system empowered ordinary citizens, allowing them to influence public policy and hold officials accountable. The democratic principles of Athens laid the groundwork for modern democratic systems and highlighted the importance of civic participation and public debate.

Education, Philosophy, and Famous Philosophers

Education in Athens aimed to cultivate well-rounded citizens. Boys received training in literacy, music, and physical education, while higher education focused on rhetoric and philosophy. Athens became a centre for philosophical thought, producing towering figures such as Socrates, Plato, and Aristotle.

Socrates

Socrates (470-399 BCE) was a seminal figure in Western philosophy, known for his method of questioning, the Socratic Method, which sought to stimulate critical thinking and illuminate ideas through dialogue. Despite leaving no written works, his teachings were recorded by his student Plato. Socrates emphasized the importance of ethics and the pursuit of virtue, questioning the conventional wisdom of his time and urging individuals to seek knowledge and self-awareness.

Plato

Plato (427-347 BCE), a student of Socrates, founded the Academy in Athens, one of the earliest institutions of higher learning. His works, written in the form of dialogues, explore a wide range of philosophical topics, including ethics, politics, metaphysics, and epistemology. In "The Republic," Plato presents his vision of an ideal society governed by philosopher-kings, emphasizing the role of justice and the philosopher's duty to seek truth and knowledge.

Aristotle

Aristotle (384-322 BCE), a student of Plato, made significant contributions to numerous fields, including logic, biology, ethics, and politics. He founded the Lyceum, another influential educational institution. Aristotle's works, such as "Nicomachean Ethics" and "Politics," examine human behaviour, the nature of the good life, and the structure of political communities. His empirical approach to studying the natural world laid the foundations for the scientific method.

Olympic Games and Sports

The Olympic Games, held every four years in Olympia, were a vital aspect of Greek culture, celebrating physical prowess and fostering unity among the Greek city-states. The Games included various athletic competitions, such as running, wrestling, boxing, and chariot racing. Victorious athletes gained immense honor and prestige, often receiving statues and lifelong privileges in their home cities.

The Olympics also had religious significance, as they were held in honour of Zeus, the chief god of the Greek pantheon. The event included sacrifices and rituals, reinforcing the connection between physical excellence and divine favour. The tradition of the Olympic Games has endured through the centuries, evolving into the modern international event we know today.

Achievements and Contributions

Architectural Styles: Doric, Ionic, and Corinthian Columns

Greek architecture is renowned for its distinct styles and enduring aesthetic principles. Three primary architectural orders—Doric, Ionic, and Corinthian—exemplify the evolution of Greek architectural design.

Doric Order

The Doric order is the oldest and simplest of the three, characterized by sturdy, fluted columns with plain, saucer- shaped capitals and no base. The Parthenon in Athens, dedicated to the goddess Athena, is a prime example of Doric architecture. The Doric style reflects a sense of strength and simplicity, embodying the austere values of the early Greek city-states.

Ionic Order

The Ionic order is more ornate than the Doric, featuring columns with bases and scrolled capitals (volutes). The columns are slenderer and more elegant, often associated with buildings in the eastern Greek islands and Asia Minor. The Erechtheion on the Acropolis of Athens, with its distinctive Caryatids (sculpted female figures serving as columns), is a notable example of Ionic architecture.

Corinthian Order

The Corinthian order is the most elaborate, distinguished by slender fluted columns and intricate capitals adorned with acanthus leaves. This style became popular during the Hellenistic period and was widely adopted by the Romans. The Temple of Olympian Zeus in Athens showcases the grandeur and decorative complexity of the Corinthian order.

Literature: Homer's "Iliad" and "Odyssey"

Greek literature has had a profound impact on Western culture, with Homer's epic poems, the "Iliad" and the "Odyssey," standing as cornerstones of ancient literary tradition.

The Iliad

The "Iliad" is an epic poem set during the Trojan War, focusing on the hero Achilles and the themes of honor, wrath, and fate. Through its vivid characters and dramatic narrative, the "Iliad" explores the human condition, the nature of heroism, and the consequences of war. Its portrayal of the interplay between gods and humans highlights the ancient Greek belief in divine intervention and the capriciousness of fate.

The Odyssey

The "Odyssey" follows the journey of Odysseus as he returns home from the Trojan War, facing numerous trials and adventures along the way. Themes of perseverance, cunning, and the quest for home resonate throughout the narrative. The "Odyssey" also delves into the complexities of human relationships, the power of intellect, and the enduring struggle against adversity.

Homer's epics not only provided entertainment and moral instruction but also served as foundational texts for Greek education and cultural identity. They influenced subsequent literature, inspiring countless adaptations, and reinterpretations across various artistic forms.

Scientific Discoveries and Contributions

Ancient Greece was a hotbed of scientific inquiry and discovery, laying the groundwork for many modern scientific disciplines. Greek thinkers approached the natural world with curiosity and a desire to understand its underlying principles through observation and reason.

Mathematics

Greek mathematicians made significant advancements in geometry and number theory. Euclid, often referred to as the "father of geometry," wrote "Elements," a comprehensive treatise that systematized the principles of geometry and served as a standard textbook for centuries. Pythagoras, known for the Pythagorean theorem, explored the relationships between numbers and their properties, influencing mathematical thought profoundly.

Astronomy

Greek astronomers made groundbreaking observations and theories about the cosmos. Hipparchus developed a system for cataloguing stars and calculating their positions, laying the foundations for modern astronomy. Ptolemy's work, the "Almagest," synthesized astronomical knowledge and proposed a geocentric model of the universe that dominated scientific thought for over a thousand years.

Medicine

Greek physicians, such as Hippocrates, known as the "father of medicine," sought to understand and treat illnesses through natural explanations and empirical observation. The Hippocratic Corpus, a collection of medical texts, emphasized the importance of clinical observation and ethical practices in medicine. Hippocrates advocated for a rational approach to disease, focusing on the balance of bodily fluids (humors) and the environment's impact on health. This holistic perspective marked a significant departure from supernatural explanations of illness and laid the groundwork for modern medical science.

Another prominent figure, Galen, built upon Hippocratic principles and made extensive contributions to anatomy and physiology. His dissections of animals advanced the understanding of the human body's structure and function, and his writings influenced medical practice in both the Western and Islamic worlds for many centuries.

Philosophy and Scientific Thought

Philosophers like Socrates, Plato, and Aristotle did not confine their inquiries to metaphysics and ethics but also delved into natural philosophy, which encompassed early scientific investigation.

Socratic Method and Ethics

Socrates introduced the Socratic method, a form of cooperative argumentative dialogue that stimulates critical thinking and illuminates ideas through questioning. His focus on ethics and the examination of moral concepts influenced Western philosophical thought profoundly.

Plato's Idealism

Plato, a student of Socrates, explored the nature of reality through his theory of Forms, which posited that the material world is a shadow of a higher, immutable reality.

In works like "The Republic," Plato examined the nature of justice, the ideal state, and the philosopher-king concept, laying the foundations for political philosophy.

Aristotle's Empiricism

Aristotle, Plato's student, made substantial contributions to logic, metaphysics, biology, and ethics. His empirical approach to studying the natural world emphasized observation and classification. Aristotle's works, such as "Nicomachean Ethics" and "Politics," provided systematic analyses of human behavior and governance, influencing subsequent scientific and philosophical inquiry.

Religion and Mythology

Religion and mythology were integral to ancient Greek life, shaping their worldview, cultural practices, and artistic expressions. The Greeks worshipped a pantheon of gods and goddesses, each with distinct personalities, domains, and mythological stories.

The Pantheon of Greek Gods and Goddesses

The Greek pantheon was led by Zeus, the king of the gods, who ruled over the sky and thunder. Other major deities included:

- **Hera:** Queen of the gods and goddess of marriage and family.
- **Poseidon:** God of the sea, earthquakes, and horses.
- **Demeter:** Goddess of agriculture and the harvest.
- **Athena:** Goddess of wisdom, warfare, and crafts.
- **Apollo:** God of the sun, music, prophecy, and healing.
- **Artemis:** Goddess of the hunt, wilderness, and childbirth.
- **Ares:** God of war.
- **Aphrodite:** Goddess of love and beauty.
- **Hephaestus:** God of fire, metalworking, and craftsmanship.
- **Hermes:** Messenger of the gods, god of trade, thieves, and travel.

- **Hestia:** Goddess of the hearth and domestic life.

These deities were believed to reside on Mount Olympus and interacted with humans, influencing their lives and destinies. Greek mythology featured rich narratives that explained natural phenomena, human behavior, and cultural traditions.

Mythological Stories and Their Impact on Culture

Greek mythology encompassed a vast array of stories that conveyed moral lessons, entertained, and explained the mysteries of the natural world. These myths were integral to Greek culture, influencing literature, art, and religious practices.

Prominent Mythological Stories

- **The Creation Myths:** Greek mythology includes various accounts of the world's creation, the gods, and humanity. The primordial deities Gaia (Earth) and Uranus (Sky) gave birth to the Titans, who were eventually overthrown by the Olympian gods led by Zeus.

- **The Twelve Labors of Heracles:** Heracles, known for his incredible strength and heroism, was tasked with completing twelve nearly impossible labors as penance. These feats, such as slaying the Nemean Lion and capturing the Golden Hind of Artemis, symbolized human perseverance and the triumph of good over evil.

- **The Trojan War:** Chronicled in Homer's "Iliad," the Trojan War was a legendary conflict between the Greeks and Trojans, sparked by the abduction of Helen by Paris. The epic explores themes of honor, wrath, and fate, with iconic characters like Achilles, Hector, and Odysseus.

- **The Odyssey:** Following the Trojan War, Odysseus' ten-year journey home to Ithaca is depicted in Homer's "Odyssey." The narrative highlights themes of cunning, endurance, and the hero's struggle against adversity.

Cultural Impact

Greek mythology permeated every aspect of Greek life, from religious rituals to artistic expressions. Temples dedicated to gods and goddesses were centers of worship and community life, adorned with sculptures and reliefs depicting mythological scenes. Festivals such as the Panathenaia in Athens celebrated deities like Athena through processions, sacrifices, and athletic competitions.

Mythological themes were also prevalent in Greek literature and drama. Tragic playwrights such as Aeschylus, Sophocles, and Euripides drew heavily from mythological sources, exploring human emotions and ethical dilemmas through their characters. Similarly, Greek art, including vase painting and sculpture, frequently illustrated mythological tales, providing visual narratives that reinforced cultural values and religious beliefs.

Conclusion

The civilization of ancient Greece was marked by its profound achievements and contributions across various fields, from philosophy and science to art and architecture. The unique geography and political fragmentation of Greece fostered the development of diverse city-states, each with its distinct cultural identity. Athens and Sparta exemplified the contrasting models of democratic governance and militaristic society, respectively, shaping the course of Greek history.

The legacy of Greek education, philosophy, and literature has had a lasting impact on Western thought, influencing subsequent generations of thinkers and scholars. The Olympic Games and Greek contributions to sports and physical culture continue to inspire and unite people worldwide.

Greek achievements in architecture, with the development of Doric, Ionic, and Corinthian styles, set enduring standards for aesthetic beauty and structural innovation. Literary works like Homer's "Iliad" and "Odyssey" remain foundational texts that explore timeless human themes and narratives.

The scientific and medical advancements of Greek thinkers laid the groundwork for modern disciplines, emphasizing observation, rational inquiry, and ethical practice. Greek religion and mythology, with their rich pantheon of gods and goddesses and compelling mythological stories, provided a framework for understanding the natural world and human existence, influencing art, literature, and cultural practices.

In conclusion, the civilization of ancient Greece, with its remarkable achievements and enduring contributions, has left an indelible mark on human history, continuing to inspire and inform our contemporary world. The legacy of ancient Greece reminds us of the heights of human creativity, intellect, and aspiration, serving as a testament to the enduring power of cultural heritage and the pursuit of knowledge.

Chapter 4
Ancient Rome

Ancient Rome, a civilization that began as a small city- state and grew into one of the most powerful empires in history, has left an indelible mark on the world. From its strategic geographical position to its remarkable expansion, the Roman Republic and Empire shaped the cultural, social, and political landscape of the ancient world. This chapter delves into the founding and expansion of Rome, its societal structures, daily life, and monumental achievements, as well as its rich religious traditions and the pivotal shift from paganism to Christianity.

Geography and Expansion

The Founding of Rome and the Roman Republic

The origins of Rome are steeped in myth and legend, with the story of Romulus and Remus being the most famous. According to this myth, the twin brothers were the sons of the god Mars and the priestess Rhea Silvia. Abandoned at birth and raised by a she-wolf, they eventually founded the city of Rome in 753 BCE. After a quarrel, Romulus killed Remus and became the first king of Rome, giving his name to the city.

Historically, the foundation of Rome is linked to the merging of several small Latin settlements on the Palatine Hill. These early settlements benefited from Rome's strategic location along the Tiber River, which provided access to trade routes and a natural defense against invasions.

The Roman Republic was established in 509 BCE after the overthrow of the last Roman king, Tarquin the Proud. This new political system was characterized by a complex form of representative democracy, with elected officials, such as consuls and senators, sharing power. The Republic's constitution evolved over time, incorporating elements of democracy, oligarchy, and monarchy, which allowed it to adapt and thrive.

The Roman Empire's Expansion and Its Impact

Rome's expansion began with the conquest of the Italian Peninsula and continued with the subjugation of the Mediterranean world and beyond.

This expansion was driven by a combination of military prowess, strategic diplomacy, and the integration of conquered peoples.

The Punic Wars: A significant milestone in Rome's expansion was the series of conflicts known as the Punic Wars, fought against Carthage. The three Punic Wars (264146BCE) culminated in the destruction of Carthage and the dominance of Rome in the western Mediterranean.

These wars showcased Rome's military capabilities and strategic acumen.

Conquests in the East: Rome's influence extended into the eastern Mediterranean through the conquest of Hellenistic kingdoms, such as Macedonia, Greece, and the remnants of Alexander the Great's empire. This expansion brought immense wealth and cultural influences, leading to a blend of Roman and Greek traditions known as Greco-Roman culture.

The Empire at Its Zenith: At its height, the Roman Empire spanned three continents, encompassing territories from Britain in the northwest to Egypt in the southeast, and from Spain in the west to the Mesopotamian border in the east. This vast empire facilitated the exchange of goods, ideas, and cultures, contributing to a period of relative peace and stability known as the Pax Romana (27 BCE -180CE).

Impact of Expansion: Rome's expansion had profound effects on its economy, society, and culture. The influx of wealth from conquered territories funded public works, such as roads, aqueducts, and temples, enhancing urban life. However, the expansion also brought challenges, including the management of diverse populations and the strain on Rome's political and administrative systems.

Society and Culture

Social Classes: Patricians, Plebeians, Slaves

Roman society was hierarchical, with distinct social classes that defined one's status, rights, and privileges.

Patricians: The patricians were the aristocratic class, descended from the original senators appointed by Romulus. They held most of the political power and large estates. Patricians occupied key religious and governmental positions and were often wealthy landowners and influential leaders.

Plebeians: The plebeians, or commoners, made up the majority of the population. They included farmers, artisans, merchants, and laborers. Over time, plebeians fought for and gained significant political rights, including the creation of the office of the Tribune of the Plebs, which allowed them to elect representatives to protect their interests against patrician dominance.

Slaves: Slavery was integral to Roman society and economy. Slaves were acquired through conquests, trade, and reproduction. They worked in households, agriculture, mines, and public projects. Despite their lack of rights, some slaves could gain freedom and citizenship, a process known as manumission.

Equestrians and Freedmen: Another notable social group was the equestrians, or knights, who were wealthy but not of aristocratic birth. They played crucial roles in commerce and military service. Freedmen, former slaves who had been granted freedom, also formed a distinct social group with limited rights but could achieve significant economic success.

Roman Law and Governance

Roman law and governance were foundational to the Republic and later the Empire, influencing legal systems for centuries to come.

The Twelve Tables: One of the earliest codifications of Roman law was the Twelve Tables, established around 450 BCE. This legal code provided a framework for public, private, and procedural law, ensuring greater transparency and fairness in the legal process.

Republican Institutions: The Roman Republic's governance was characterized by a system of checks and balances, with power divided among various offices and institutions. Key institutions included:

- **Consuls:** The highest elected officials, serving one- year terms. Two consuls shared executive power and led the army.
- **Senate:** A body of experienced statesmen, primarily from the patrician class, which advised magistrates and influenced legislation.
- **Assemblies:** Popular assemblies where citizens voted on laws, elected officials, and made key decisions. The most important were the Centuriate Assembly and the Tribal Assembly.
- **Tribunes:** Officials elected by the plebeians to protect their interests. Tribunes had the power to veto actions by magistrates and propose legislation.

Imperial Governance: The transition from Republic to Empire under Augustus introduced a more autocratic system while retaining some republican elements. The emperor held supreme power, controlling the military, judicial, and religious spheres. Despite this concentration of power, the Senate and other institutions continued to function, providing a semblance of continuity and stability.

Daily Life, Clothing, and Food

Daily life in ancient Rome varied significantly across social classes but shared common cultural and domestic practices.

Housing: Wealthy Romans lived in spacious houses (domus) with courtyards, gardens, and elaborate decorations. The poor lived in crowded apartment buildings (insulae), often facing hazardous conditions.

Clothing: Roman clothing was practical and symbolized social status. Men wore togas, while women wore stolas. Both garments were made of wool or linen. The toga was a symbol of Roman citizenship, worn over a tunic. The color and decoration of the toga indicated the wearer's rank and status.

Food: Roman cuisine was diverse, influenced by the various regions of the empire. Common foods included bread, olives, cheese, fruits, vegetables, and meat. Wealthy Romans enjoyed elaborate feasts with exotic dishes, while the poor relied on simpler meals. Wine was a staple drink for all classes.

Daily Activities: Romans engaged in various activities, from work to leisure. Public baths were popular for socializing and relaxation. The forum was the center of public life, where markets, political activities, and social gatherings took place. Entertainment included gladiatorial games, chariot races, and theatrical performances.

Achievements and Contributions

Engineering Feats: Roads, Aqueducts, and the Colosseum

Roman engineering was unparalleled, with innovations that showcased their ingenuity and practical skills.

Roads: The Romans built an extensive network of roads, facilitating military movement, trade, and communication across the empire. These roads were constructed with layers of materials for durability and included milestones and rest stations. Famous roads like the Via Appia connected Rome with distant provinces, ensuring cohesion and control.

Aqueducts: Roman aqueducts were monumental achievements in hydraulic engineering, supplying cities with fresh water. These structures, often spanning great distances, used gravity to transport water from springs and rivers. The Aqua Appia and Aqua Claudia are notable examples, demonstrating the Romans' ability to overcome geographical challenges and improve urban living conditions.

The Colosseum: The Colosseum, also known as the Flavian Amphitheater, is an iconic symbol of Roman architectural prowess. Completed in 80 CE, it could hold up to 50,000 spectators and hosted gladiatorial contests, animal hunts, and public spectacles. Its design, featuring a complex system of vaults and corridors, influenced the construction of large-scale entertainment venues for centuries.

Latin Language and Literature

Latin, the language of Rome, became the foundation for many modern languages and a medium for a rich literary tradition.

Language: Latin evolved from an Italic dialect to the dominant language of the Roman Empire. It was the language of administration, literature, and law. Classical Latin, used in formal writing and speeches, coexisted with Vulgar Latin, spoken by the common people and evolving into the Romance languages (Spanish, French, Italian, Portuguese, and Romanian).

Literature: Roman literature encompassed various genres, including epic poetry, history, philosophy, and rhetoric. Key literary figures include:

- **Virgil:** His epic poem "The Aeneid" became Rome's national epic, celebrating its origins and the virtues of duty and piety.
- **Ovid:** Known for his elegiac poetry and mythological works, such as "Metamorphoses," which influenced Western art and literature.
- **Horace:** A lyric poet whose "Odes" and "Satires" explored themes of love, friendship, and philosophy.
- **Cicero:** A statesman and orator whose speeches and philosophical works shaped Roman rhetoric and political thought.
- **Seneca:** A philosopher and playwright whose Stoic writings offered insights into ethics and human behavior.

Innovations in Government and Law

Rome's contributions to government and law laid the groundwork for modern legal systems and political thought.

Republican Ideals: The Roman Republic's blend of democratic, oligarchic, and monarchical elements provided a model for balanced governance. The concepts of checks and balances, separation of powers, and the rule of law influenced later political systems, including modern democracies.

Roman Law: Roman law was comprehensive and systematically codified, addressing civil, criminal, and administrative matters. Key developments include:

- **The Twelve Tables:** Rome's earliest legal code, ensuring transparency and equality before the law.
- **The Corpus Juris Civilis:** Compiled under Emperor Justinian in the 6th century CE, this body of civil law became the foundation for legal systems in many European countries.
- **Legal Principles:** Roman law introduced concepts such as contracts, property rights, and legal representation. The principle of "innocent until proven guilty" and the right to a fair trial were significant contributions to legal thought.

Religion and Mythology

Religion and mythology played central roles in Roman culture, reflecting both continuity with and adaptation of earlier traditions.

Roman Gods and Their Greek Counterparts

Roman religion was deeply influenced by Greek mythology, with many Roman gods directly corresponding to Greek deities.

- **Jupiter (Zeus):** King of the gods, god of the sky and thunder.
- **Juno (Hera):** Queen of the gods, goddess of marriage and childbirth.
- **Neptune (Poseidon):** God of the sea, earthquakes, and horses.

- **Minerva (Athena):** Goddess of wisdom, warfare, and crafts.
- **Mars (Ares):** God of war.
- **Venus (Aphrodite):** Goddess of love and beauty.
- **Apollo (same in both traditions):** God of the sun, music, and prophecy.
- **Diana (Artemis):** Goddess of the hunt, wilderness, and childbirth.
- **Vulcan (Hephaestus):** God of fire and metalworking.
- **Mercury (Hermes):** Messenger of the gods, god of trade and travel.
- **Ceres (Demeter):** Goddess of agriculture and the harvest.
- **Vesta (Hestia):** Goddess of the hearth and domestic life.

The Transition from Paganism to Christianity

One of the most significant cultural shifts in Roman history was the transition from traditional polytheistic beliefs to Christianity.

Early Christianity: Christianity emerged in the Roman province of Judea in the1stcentury CE. Initially, it was one of many mystery religions and faced persecution from Roman authorities. Christians were often viewed with suspicion for their refusal to worship the Roman gods and the emperor.

Constantine and the Edict of Milan: The conversion of Emperor Constantine to Christianity in the early 4th century CE marked a turning point. The Edict of Milan in313CE legalized Christianity and granted religious tolerance throughout the empire. Constantine's support for Christianity included patronage of church-building projects and convening the First Council of Nicaea in 325 CE, which sought to unify Christian doctrine.

Theodosius and the Establishment of Christianity: In 380 CE, Emperor Theodosius I made Christianity the official state religion of the Roman Empire with the Edict of Thessalonica. Pagan practices were increasingly suppressed, and Christian institutions became integral to Roman state and society.

Impact on Roman Culture: The adoption of Christianity transformed Roman cultural and religious life. Pagan temples were repurposed as churches, and Christian symbolism permeated art and architecture. The shift also influenced legal and social norms, with Christian ethics shaping policies on issues like slavery, charity, and family life.

Conclusion

The civilization of ancient Rome, from its legendary founding to its vast empire, made monumental contributions to human history. Rome's strategic geographical position facilitated its rise and expansion, impacting societies across Europe, Asia, and Africa.

Roman society was marked by a complex hierarchy, with distinct social classes and a legal system that emphasized the rule of law and the rights of citizens. Daily life in Rome varied widely, reflecting the diversity and wealth of the empire.

Roman achievements in engineering, literature, and law set enduring standards that influenced subsequent civilizations. The construction of roads, aqueducts, and monumental structures like the Colosseum showcased Roman ingenuity and practical skills. Latin language and literature enriched cultural expression and communication, while Roman law provided a foundation for modern legal systems.

Religion and mythology were integral to Roman identity, evolving from polytheistic traditions to the widespread adoption of Christianity. This religious transformation had profound effects on Roman culture and laid the groundwork for the development of Western civilization.

Ancient Rome's legacy continues to resonate in contemporary society, reminding us of the enduring impact of its innovations, governance, and cultural achievements.

Chapter 5
The Indus Valley Civilization

The Indus Valley Civilization, one of the world's earliest urban cultures, flourished around 3300 to1300BCE in the northwestern regions of South Asia. Known for its advanced urban planning, sophisticated architecture, and undeciphered script, the civilization offers profound insights into early human societies. This chapter explores the geography and early settlements, societal structure and culture, remarkable achievements, and religious beliefs of the Indus Valley Civilization, and their connections to later Indian culture and religion.

Geography and Early Settlements

The Importance of the Indus River

The Indus Valley Civilization owed much of its development and sustenance to the Indus River and its tributaries. The river provided a reliable source of water for agriculture, enabling the growth of surplus crops, which supported large urban populations. The fertile plains of the Indus River basin allowed for the cultivation of wheat, barley, peas, and other crops, essential for sustaining the civilization's cities and trade networks.

The river also facilitated transportation and trade, linking the cities of the Indus Valley with other contemporary civilizations, including Mesopotamia and ancient Egypt. The seasonal flooding of the Indus River deposited rich silt on the surrounding lands, enhancing agricultural productivity and supporting the growth of cities like Harappa and Mohenjo-Daro.

Major Cities: Harappa and Mohenjo-Daro

Harappa: Harappa, located in present-day Punjab, Pakistan, is one of the principal cities of the Indus Valley Civilization. The site, excavated in the early 20th century, revealed a well-planned urban center with advanced infrastructure, including granaries, drainage systems, and fortified administrative centers. Harappa's layout suggests a high degree of social organization and administrative control, with wide streets arranged in a grid pattern and standardized brick sizes indicating sophisticated construction techniques.

Mohenjo-Daro: Mohenjo-Daro, situated in the Sindh province of Pakistan, is another major urban center of the Indus Valley Civilization. Discovered in the 1920s, this site is renowned for its exceptional urban planning and architectural feats. Mohenjo-Daro featured a central citadel, large public baths, residential areas, and an elaborate drainage system. The Great Bath, a large, watertight pool built from bricks and bitumen, is particularly notable, suggesting the significance of ritualistic or communal bathing in the culture.

Both Harappa and Mohenjo-Daro exemplify the advanced state of urban development in the Indus Valley Civilization, with their well-organized layouts, standardized building practices, and sophisticated public amenities reflecting a high degree of social complexity and administrative efficiency.

Society and Culture

Urban Planning and Advanced Drainage Systems

One of the most remarkable aspects of the Indus Valley Civilization is its urban planning. Cities like Harappa and Mohenjo-Daro were meticulously laid out, reflecting a well-thought-out approach to urban development. Streets were aligned in a grid pattern, with major thoroughfares intersecting at right angles, facilitating organized movement and trade.

Drainage Systems: The Indus cities featured advanced drainage systems unparalleled in the ancient world. Houses were connected to a network of covered drains, which ran alongside the streets, ensuring efficient disposal of waste water and preventing flooding during the monsoon season. This system indicates a high level of public health awareness and civic management, emphasizing the importance placed on hygiene and urban cleanliness.

Public Buildings and Granaries: The presence of large granaries in cities like Harappa and Mohenjo-Daro suggests centralized control of food storage and distribution, essential for supporting urban populations. Public buildings, including assembly halls and market areas, indicate organized civic activities and a structured approach to governance.

Social Organization and Daily Life

The social structure of the Indus Valley Civilization, while not fully understood, appears to have been complex and stratified. Archaeological evidence suggests a well- organized society with distinct social classes, possibly including merchants, artisans, farmers, and administrators.

Residential Areas: Housing in the Indus cities ranged from large, multi-roomed dwellings for the elite to smaller, more modest houses for the common people. The uniformity in brick sizes and construction techniques across different housing types suggests standardization and possibly state control over building practices.

Daily Life: Daily life in the Indus Valley cities would have been bustling, with markets, workshops, and public spaces filled with activity. People engaged in various crafts, including pottery, bead-making, metallurgy, and textiles. The widespread use of standardized weights and measures indicates a well-regulated economic system, facilitating trade and commerce.

Clothing and Adornments: The inhabitants of the Indus Valley Civilization wore simple yet functional clothing, likely made from cotton and wool. Men and women adorned themselves with jewelry made from gold, silver, and semi-precious stones, showcasing their skills in metallurgy and craftsmanship. The discovery of numerous figurines and sculptures also suggests a rich tradition of artistic expression.

Achievements and Contributions

Writing System and Undeciphered Script

One of the most intriguing aspects of the Indus Valley Civilization is its writing system, which remains undeciphered to this day. Thousands of inscribed seals and pottery shards have been discovered, featuring a script that consists of approximately 400 distinct symbols. Despite extensive research, the script's exact nature and the language it represents remain a mystery.

Seals and Inscriptions: The seals, often made of steatite, depict animals, humans, and various symbols, likely used for trade, administrative purposes, or identification. The undeciphered script on these seals suggests a form of written communication and record-keeping, integral to the civilization's economic and administrative functions.

Challenges in Decipherment: The lack of a bilingual inscription (akin to the Rosetta Stone for Egyptian hieroglyphs) and the brevity of most inscriptions have made deciphering the script challenging. Scholars continue to debate whether it represents a proto- Dravidian language, an early Indo-Aryan language, or another language entirely.

Trade and Economy

The Indus Valley Civilization was a hub of trade and economic activity, with evidence of extensive trade networks both within the region and with distant lands.

Internal Trade: The standardized weights and measures found throughout the Indus cities suggest a highly regulated trade system. Markets and workshops indicate a thriving local economy, with goods such as pottery, beads, textiles, and metalwork being produced and exchanged.

External Trade: Archaeological evidence points to trade links with Mesopotamia, the Persian Gulf, and possibly Egypt. Indus Valley seals and artifacts have been found in these regions, indicating the exchange of goods such as textiles, pottery, and precious materials. The trade networks facilitated cultural exchange and the diffusion of technologies and ideas.

Craftsmanship and Industry: The Indus Valley people excelled in various crafts, including bead-making, metallurgy, pottery, and textiles. The production of high- quality goods for both domestic use and trade showcases their advanced technological skills and aesthetic sensibilities. The discovery of standardized tools and techniques across different sites suggests a high degree of specialization and organization in their industries.

Artistic and Craft Achievements

The artistic achievements of the Indus Valley Civilization reflect their advanced skills in various crafts and their aesthetic sensibilities.

Pottery: Indus pottery is characterized by its fine quality and intricate designs. Painted motifs, often depicting animals, plants, and geometric patterns, showcase the artisans' creativity and technical prowess. The pottery was both functional and decorative, used in daily life and for ritual purposes.

Bead-Making: The Indus people were renowned for their bead-making skills, producing beads from materials such as carnelian, agate, and lapis lazuli. These beads were used in jewelry, trade, and possibly as status symbols. The intricate techniques employed in bead production, including drilling and polishing, highlight their technological advancements.

Sculpture and Figurines: Numerous figurines and sculptures have been discovered, depicting animals, humans, and deities. The famous "Dancing Girl" bronze statue from Mohenjo-Daro is a testament to their skill in metalwork and their ability to capture dynamic movement in art.

Terracotta figurines of animals and humans suggest religious or cultural significance, possibly used in rituals or as toys.

Religion and Beliefs

Possible Religious Practices and Deities

The religious beliefs and practices of the Indus Valley Civilization remain largely speculative due to the lack of deciphered texts. However, archaeological evidence provides some insights into their spiritual life.

Seals and Symbols: Many Indus seals depict animals, mythological creatures, and human figures, possibly representing deities or religious motifs. The recurring image of a figure seated in a yogic posture, often identified as Proto-Shiva or Pashupati, suggests the worship of a deity associated with animals and fertility.

The Great Bath: The presence of large public baths, such as the Great Bath in Mohenjo-Daro, indicates the significance of ritual purification and communal bathing in their religious practices. These structures suggest that water held a central role in their spiritual and social life.

Terracotta Figurines: Numerous terracotta figurines of female figures, often interpreted as mother goddesses, suggest the worship of fertility and nature deities. These figurines indicate a possible focus on fertility rites and the veneration of feminine aspects of divinity.

Connections to Later Indian Culture and Religion

The religious practices and beliefs of the Indus Valley Civilization likely influenced later Indian culture and religious traditions.

Continuity and Influence: Elements of Indus Valley religion, such as the worship of nature deities, ritual bathing, and possibly early forms of yoga, may have persisted and evolved into the Vedic and later Hindu traditions. The emphasis on purification, fertility, and the worship of deities associated with natural elements finds echoes in the later Vedic rituals and Hindu practices.

Proto-Shiva and Pashupati: The depiction of a deity in a yogic posture on Indus seals bears resemblance to later depictions of Shiva as Pashupati (Lord of Animals) and the yogic ascetic. This continuity suggests that aspects of Indus Valley spirituality contributed to the formation of later Hindu deities and religious concepts.

Urban Planning and Vastu Shastra: The advanced urban planning and architectural principles of the Indus Valley may have influenced the development of Vastu Shastra, the ancient Indian science of architecture and urban planning. The emphasis on harmonious layouts and the use of standardized construction techniques reflect early insights into spatial organization and environmental harmony.

Conclusion

The Indus Valley Civilization, with its remarkable urban planning, advanced infrastructure, and rich cultural heritage, represents a pinnacle of early human achievement. Its sophisticated cities, standardized practices, and intricate crafts highlight the complexity and innovation of this ancient society.

Despite the challenges in deciphering their script and fully understanding their social and religious structures, the legacy of the Indus Valley Civilization continues to intrigue and inspire scholars and enthusiasts alike. The civilization's contributions to urban planning, craftsmanship, and possibly early religious practices have left an indelible mark on the history of human development.

As we explore the depths of this ancient civilization, we gain valuable insights into the ingenuity, resilience, and creativity of our early ancestors, reminding us of the enduring impact of the Indus Valley on the tapestry of human history.

Chapter 6
Ancient Persia

The Persian Empire, known for its grandeur and extensive reach, was a powerful and influential civilization that spanned several centuries and continents. This chapter delves into the geography and early settlements of the Persian Empire, its society and culture, significant achievements, and the profound impact of its religion and mythology.

Geography and Early Settlement

Location and Expansion of the Persian Empire

The Persian Empire, at its zenith, was the largest empire the ancient world had ever seen, encompassing diverse regions and cultures. It extended from the Indus Valley in the east to the Aegean Sea in the west, and from the Caucasus and Central Asia in the north to Egypt and the Arabian Peninsula in the south.

Geographical Diversity: The empire's vast expanse included various geographical features, such as the fertile plains of Mesopotamia, the arid deserts of Iran, the mountainous regions of Anatolia, and the lush river valleys of Egypt. This diversity required innovative administrative strategies to manage and integrate the different regions effectively.

Founding and Early Expansion: The roots of the Persian Empire trace back to the region of Pars (Fars) in southwestern Iran. The Persians, an Indo-European people, settled in this region around the 10th century BCE.

Under the leadership of Cyrus the Great (Cyrus II), the Persian Empire began its rapid expansion in the mid-6th century BCE. Cyrus's conquests included the Median Empire, the Lydian Kingdom, and the Neo-Babylonian Empire, establishing Persian dominance across a vast territory.

Achaemenid Dynasty: The Achaemenid Dynasty, founded by Cyrus the Great, marked the first Persian Empire. Subsequent rulers, such as Darius the Great and Xerxes, continued to expand and consolidate the empire, implementing effective administrative systems and building impressive infrastructure.

Key Cities and Regions

Persepolis: Persepolis, the ceremonial capital of the Achaemenid Empire, is one of the most iconic cities of ancient Persia. Founded by Darius the Great, Persepolis was a symbol of the empire's grandeur and architectural sophistication. The city hosted grand ceremonies, including the New Year festival (Nowruz), and served as a hub for administration and governance.

Susa: Susa, one of the oldest cities in the world, was another major city of the Persian Empire. It served as an administrative capital and a strategic center for communication and trade. The city's location in the fertile plains of Elam made it a critical link between the Persian heartland and the western provinces.

Pasargadae: Pasargadae, the first capital of the Achaemenid Empire, was established by Cyrus the Great. It is known for its impressive architectural features, including Cyrus's tomb and the Royal Garden, which exemplified early Persian garden design.

Ecbatana: Ecbatana (modern Hamadan) was the capital of the Median Empire and later an important city in the Persian Empire. Its strategic location in the Zagros Mountains made it a vital military and administrative center.

Other Key Regions: The Persian Empire included many other significant regions, such as Anatolia, Mesopotamia, Egypt, and parts of Central Asia. Each region contributed to the empire's cultural and economic diversity, enriching Persian civilization.

Society and Culture

Social Hierarchy: Kings, Satraps, Nobles, Commoners, and Slaves

The Persian Empire had a well-defined social hierarchy that structured its vast and diverse society.

The King: At the top of the social hierarchy was the king, who held absolute power and was considered divinely appointed. The king's authority was supported by a bureaucratic system and loyal nobility. Persian kings, such as Cyrus the Great, Darius the Great, and Xerxes, were celebrated for their leadership and military prowess.

Satraps: The empire was divided into provinces called satrapies, each governed by a satrap. Satraps were usually members of the royal family or high-ranking nobles. They were responsible for collecting taxes, maintaining law and order, and protecting the province from external threats. The satraps' loyalty to the king was ensured through a system of checks and balances, including royal inspectors known as the "King's Eyes and Ears."

Nobles: Persian nobles held significant power and wealth. They owned large estates, commanded military units, and served in the royal court. Nobles played a crucial role in the administration and military operations of the empire.

Commoners: The common people included farmers, artisans, merchants, and laborers. They formed the backbone of the economy, producing goods, paying taxes, and serving in the military. Commoners had some degree of social mobility, especially those who excelled in their professions or demonstrated loyalty to the state.

Slaves: Slavery existed in ancient Persia, though it was not as widespread as in some other ancient civilizations. Slaves were typically prisoners of war or debtors. They worked in households, agriculture, and public projects. Despite their low status, slaves could sometimes earn their freedom and integrate into society.

Daily Life and Customs

Daily life in the Persian Empire varied greatly depending on one's social status, occupation, and region.

Housing and Architecture: Persian homes ranged from simple mud-brick houses for commoners to grand palaces for the nobility. Urban areas featured well-planned streets, markets, and public buildings. Persian architecture was renowned for its use of columns, intricate stone carvings, and grandiose structures like the palaces at Persepolis and Susa.

Clothing and Adornments: Persian clothing was influenced by both practicality and status. Men typically wore tunics and trousers, while women wore long dresses. Both genders adorned themselves with jewelry made from gold, silver, and precious stones. Clothing and adornments often indicated social status, with nobility wearing more elaborate and richly decorated attire.

Food and Diet: The Persian diet included a variety of grains, fruits, vegetables, meat, and dairy products. Bread and barley were staples, while dates, pomegranates, and melons were popular fruits. Meat, including lamb, goat, and poultry, was often consumed during festivals and special occasions. The Persians were also known for their wine and the cultivation of spices.

Entertainment and Leisure: Persians enjoyed various forms of entertainment, including music, dance, hunting, and board games. Banquets and feasts were common, often featuring music, poetry, and storytelling. The Persians also valued physical fitness and participated in sports such as archery, horseback riding, and wrestling.

Art and Architecture

Persian art and architecture reflect the empire's grandeur and cultural diversity. Influences from different regions and civilizations were integrated into a unique Persian style.

Architecture: Persian architecture is characterized by its monumental scale, intricate decorations, and innovative engineering. Key features include:

- **Palaces and Temples:** The palaces of Persepolis and Susa exemplify Persian architectural brilliance, with their grand halls, extensive use of columns, and detailed reliefs depicting royal ceremonies and battles. Temples and ziggurats, such as those in Susa, highlight the religious aspects of Persian architecture.

- **Gardens:** Persian gardens, known as "paradises," were meticulously designed with geometric layouts, water channels, and lush vegetation. These gardens symbolized paradise on earth and influenced garden design in later Islamic and Western cultures.

- **Infrastructure:** Persian engineers built extensive road networks, bridges, and aqueducts, facilitating communication, trade, and administration across the vast empire.

Art: Persian art includes a wide range of media, from pottery and metalwork to sculpture and textiles. Key aspects include:

- **Reliefs and Sculptures:** The reliefs at Persepolis depict scenes of royal audiences, processions, and tributes from various subject nations. These artworks convey the power and diversity of the empire.

- **Pottery and Metalwork:** Persian artisans produced finely crafted pottery, often decorated with intricate patterns and glazes. Metalwork, including gold and silver vessels, jewelry, and weapons, showcased their skill in metallurgy and design.

- **Textiles:** Persian textiles, particularly carpets and tapestries, were renowned for their quality and intricate designs. These textiles were highly valued and traded across the ancient world.

Achievements and Contributions

Administrative Systems and Governance

The Persian Empire's administrative system was one of its most significant achievements, allowing it to manage its vast and diverse territories effectively.

Centralized Administration: The empire was divided into satrapies, each governed by a satrap who acted as the king's representative. This system allowed for efficient local governance while maintaining central control. Satraps were responsible for collecting taxes, enforcing laws, and defending their regions.

The King's Eyes and Ears: To ensure loyalty and prevent rebellion, the Persian kings employed a network of inspectors known as the "King's Eyes and Ears." These officials traveled throughout the empire, reporting directly to the king on the activities of satraps and local governors.

Legal System: The Persian legal system combined local customs with imperial decrees. Laws were codified and enforced by local judges, with the king serving as the ultimate judicial authority. The system aimed to be fair and just, promoting stability and order within the empire.

Taxation and Economy: The Persian Empire implemented a standardized taxation system, which provided the revenue necessary to support its vast administrative and military apparatus. Taxes were collected in various forms, including grain, livestock, and precious metals. The empire also encouraged trade and commerce, standardizing weights and measures to facilitate economic activity.

Infrastructure: Roads and Postal Systems

The Persian Empire is renowned for its impressive infrastructure, which facilitated communication, trade, and military movement across its vast territories.

Royal Road: The Royal Road, stretching over 2,500 kilometers from Sardis in Anatolia to Susa in Persia, was a major achievement of Persian engineering. It allowed for rapid communication and movement of troops, with relay stations and rest stops positioned along the route. Couriers could travel the length of the road in a matter of days, significantly enhancing administrative efficiency.

Postal System: The Persians developed an efficient postal system, with relay stations and couriers ensuring the swift transmission of messages across the empire. This system, known as the "Angarium," enabled the king and his officials to maintain control and coordination over distant regions.

Bridges and Aqueducts: Persian engineers built numerous bridges and aqueducts, showcasing their advanced understanding of hydraulics and construction. These structures facilitated the movement of people and goods and provided reliable water supplies to cities and agricultural areas.

Advances in Art and Science

The Persian Empire made significant contributions to art, science, and technology, influencing later cultures and civilizations.

Astronomy and Mathematics: Persian scholars made advances in astronomy and mathematics, building on the knowledge of earlier Mesopotamian and Greek civilizations. They developed accurate calendars, improved methods for observing celestial bodies, and made significant contributions to algebra and geometry.

Medicine: Persian physicians, such as those in the court of Darius the Great, were renowned for their medical knowledge and practices. They combined herbal remedies, surgical techniques, and an understanding of anatomy to treat various ailments. Persian medical knowledge influenced later Islamic and Western medicine.

Philosophy and Literature: Persian philosophy and literature flourished during the empire, with works such as the Avesta (the sacred texts of Zoroastrianism) and epic poetry celebrating the deeds of kings and heroes. Persian literature influenced the development of later Persian and Islamic literary traditions.

Art and Architecture: As previously mentioned, Persian art and architecture were highly advanced, combining elements from various cultures to create a unique and influential style. Persian artisans and architects set standards in craftsmanship and design that were emulated by subsequent civilizations.

Religion and Mythology

Zoroastrianism and Its Beliefs

Zoroastrianism, the predominant religion of the Persian Empire, played a crucial role in shaping its culture, governance, and worldview.

Origins and Founder: Zoroastrianism is believed to have been founded by the prophet Zoroaster (Zarathustra) around the 6th century BCE. Zoroaster's teachings, as recorded in the Avesta, emphasized the worship of Ahura Mazda, the supreme god, and the cosmic struggle between good and evil.

Core Beliefs: Zoroastrianism is a dualistic religion, centered on the conflict between Ahura Mazda (the god of light, truth, and goodness) and Angra Mainyu (Ahriman, the spirit of darkness, deceit, and evil). Followers are encouraged to live righteous lives, supporting truth and order (asha) while opposing falsehood and chaos (druj).

Ethical Principles: Zoroastrianism promotes the principles of good thoughts, good words, and good deeds. These ethical guidelines influence every aspect of a believer's life, from personal conduct to social and political responsibilities.

Afterlife and Eschatology: Zoroastrianism teaches that individuals are judged after death based on their actions during life. The souls of the righteous are rewarded with paradise, while the wicked face punishment. The religion also includes beliefs in a final renovation of the world (Frashokereti), where good ultimately triumphs over evil, and all souls are purified.

Major Gods and Religious Texts

Ahura Mazda: Ahura Mazda is the supreme god in Zoroastrianism, embodying truth, light, and goodness. He is the creator of the universe and the source of all that is good.

Angra Mainyu (Ahriman): Angra Mainyu is the malevolent spirit opposing Ahura Mazda. He represents darkness, deceit, and chaos, and is responsible for all evil and suffering in the world.

Other Divinities: Zoroastrianism also recognizes several other divinities, known as yazatas, who assist Ahura Mazda in maintaining order. These include Mithra (the god of covenant and truth), Anahita (the goddess of waters and fertility), and Sraosha (the divine messenger and protector of humanity).

Avesta: The Avesta is the sacred scripture of Zoroastrianism, containing hymns (Gathas) attributed to Zoroaster, liturgical texts, prayers, and ritual instructions. The Avesta provides guidance on religious practices, ethical conduct, and the cosmological beliefs of Zoroastrianism.

Influence on Other Religions

Zoroastrianism had a profound impact on the religious and philosophical traditions of other cultures and civilizations.

Judaism and Christianity: Scholars suggest that Zoroastrianism influenced Judaism during the Babylonian Exile and the subsequent Persian period. Concepts such as the dualistic struggle between good and evil, the idea of a messiah, and the resurrection of the dead have parallels in Zoroastrianism. These ideas were later incorporated into Christianity, shaping its theological framework.

Islam: Zoroastrianism also influenced early Islamic thought. The emphasis on monotheism, the struggle between good and evil, and ethical conduct in Zoroastrianism resonated with Islamic teachings. The integration of Persian administrative practices and cultural elements into the Islamic Caliphate further facilitated this exchange.

Manichaeism: Founded by the prophet Mani in the 3rd century CE, Manichaeism was heavily influenced by Zoroastrian dualism. It combined elements of Zoroastrianism, Christianity, and Buddhism, creating a syncretic religion that spread across the ancient world.

Conclusion

The Persian Empire, with its vast territories, sophisticated administrative systems, and rich cultural heritage, was a beacon of ancient civilization. Its contributions to art, science, architecture, and governance left an enduring legacy that influenced subsequent cultures and civilizations.

The social structure of the Persian Empire, with its well- defined hierarchy and efficient administration, ensured the stability and prosperity of its diverse regions. Daily life in the empire was marked by a blend of cultural practices, reflecting the integration of various traditions and customs.

Persian achievements in infrastructure, such as the Royal Road and postal system, facilitated communication and trade across the empire, enhancing its economic and political cohesion. Advances in art and science showcased the empire's intellectual and creative prowess, setting standards for future generations.

Zoroastrianism, as the dominant religion of the Persian Empire, shaped its cultural and ethical landscape. Its beliefs in the cosmic struggle between good and evil, ethical conduct, and the afterlife influenced later religious and philosophical traditions, leaving a lasting impact on the spiritual history of humanity.

As we explore the rich tapestry of the Persian Empire, we gain a deeper understanding of its contributions to human civilization and the enduring legacy of its cultural and intellectual achievements. The story of ancient Persia is a testament to the ingenuity, resilience, and vision of its people, whose influence continues to resonate through the corridors of history.

Chapter 7
Ancient Mesopotamia

Ancient Mesopotamia, often referred to as the "Cradle of Civilization," was a region rich in cultural and technological advancements. This chapter explores the geography and early settlement of Mesopotamia, its society and culture, significant achievements, and the profound impact of its religion and mythology.

Geography and Early Settlement

Location Between the Tigris and Euphrates Rivers

Mesopotamia, located in the modern-day Middle East, encompassed the region between the Tigris and Euphrates rivers. This fertile area, known as the Fertile Crescent, was ideal for agriculture and became the birthplace of some of the earliest human civilizations.

Geographical Features: The Tigris and Euphrates rivers provided essential water sources for irrigation, supporting agriculture and the growth of settlements. The region's flat plains facilitated the development of extensive irrigation systems, which allowed for surplus food production and the rise of complex societies.

Climate and Agriculture: The climate of Mesopotamia was characterized by hot, dry summers and mild, wet winters. This climate, combined with the fertile alluvial soil deposited by the rivers, made the region highly productive for farming. Early Mesopotamians cultivated barley, wheat, dates, and various vegetables, supporting a growing population.

Early Settlements: The favorable conditions in Mesopotamia led to the establishment of early settlements around 5000 BCE. These settlements gradually evolved into city-states, each with its own governance and cultural practices. The most notable of these early city-states were Sumer, Akkad, Babylon, and Assyria.

Early City-States: Sumer, Akkad, Babylon, and Assyria

Sumer: Sumer, located in southern Mesopotamia, is considered one of the world's first civilizations. The Sumerians developed advanced urban centers, such as Uruk, Ur, and Eridu. They are credited with the invention of cuneiform writing, the development of the wheel, and the establishment of the first known legal codes.

Akkad: The Akkadian Empire, founded by Sargon of Akkad around 2334 BCE, was the first empire to unite the city- states of Mesopotamia under a single ruler. The Akkadians adopted many aspects of Sumerian culture, including cuneiform writing, while also contributing to the development of art and military organization.

Babylon: Babylon, located in central Mesopotamia, rose to prominence under the rule of Hammurabi in the 18th century BCE. Hammurabi is best known for his comprehensive legal code, the Code of Hammurabi, which established principles of justice and social order. Babylon later became a center of learning and culture under Nebuchadnezzar II.

Assyria: Assyria, located in northern Mesopotamia, emerged as a powerful empire known for its military prowess and administrative efficiency. The Assyrians built a vast empire through conquest and maintained control through a network of provinces and governors. They are also known for their impressive architectural achievements, such as the palaces of Nineveh and Ashur.

Society and Culture

Social Structure: Kings, Priests, Merchants, Artisans, and Farmers

The social structure of ancient Mesopotamia was hierarchical, with distinct classes based on occupation, wealth, and power.

Kings: At the top of the social hierarchy were the kings, who were considered divine or semi-divine figures. They were responsible for maintaining order, administering justice, and leading military campaigns. The king's authority was often legitimized by religious beliefs, linking the ruler to the gods.

Priests: Priests held significant power and influence in Mesopotamian society. They oversaw religious rituals, managed temple economies, and served as intermediaries between the gods and the people. Temples were central to urban life, functioning as religious, economic, and administrative hubs.

Merchants and Artisans: Merchants and artisans formed the middle class of Mesopotamian society. Merchants engaged in trade, facilitating the exchange of goods and resources both within and beyond Mesopotamia. Artisans produced a wide range of goods, including pottery, textiles, metalwork, and tools, contributing to the economy and cultural life.

Farmers: The majority of the population were farmers who worked the land to produce food. They formed the backbone of Mesopotamian society, supplying the surplus that supported urban centers and specialized professions. Farmers often lived in rural villages but were subject to the authority of urban rulers and temple officials.

Daily Life and Urban Development

Daily life in ancient Mesopotamia was shaped by the social structure, economic activities, and cultural practices of the time.

Housing and Architecture: Housing in Mesopotamia varied according to social status. Commoners lived in modest mud-brick houses, while the wealthy and powerful resided in larger, more elaborate homes. Urban centers featured well-planned streets, marketplaces, and public buildings. The use of mud bricks and the development of complex construction techniques allowed for the creation of impressive structures, including ziggurats and palaces.

Clothing and Adornments: Clothing in Mesopotamia was made from wool and linen. Men typically wore tunics and skirts, while women wore long dresses. Both men and women adorned themselves with jewelry made from gold, silver, and semi-precious stones. Clothing and adornments often indicated social status and wealth.

Food and Diet: The Mesopotamian diet was diverse, including grains (barley and wheat), legumes, vegetables, fruits (dates, figs, and pomegranates), and meat (fish, poultry, and livestock). Bread and beer were staples of the diet, with beer often consumed as a nutritious and safe alternative to water.

Entertainment and Leisure: Mesopotamians enjoyed various forms of entertainment, including music, dance, board games (such as the Royal Game of Ur), and storytelling. Festivals and religious ceremonies were important social events, bringing communities together to celebrate and honor the gods.

Education and Literacy: Education was primarily the domain of the elite, with scribes receiving training in cuneiform writing and administrative skills. Schools, often attached to temples, provided instruction in writing, mathematics, and literature. Literacy was highly valued and essential for maintaining records, conducting trade, and administering the state.

Contributions to Art and Literature

Ancient Mesopotamia made significant contributions to art and literature, reflecting the creativity and intellectual achievements of its people.

Art: Mesopotamian art includes a wide range of media, from pottery and sculpture to metalwork and textiles. Notable features include:

- **Sculpture:** Mesopotamian sculptures often depicted gods, kings, and mythological scenes. Statuettes, reliefs, and monumental statues showcased the skill and craftsmanship of Mesopotamian artists.

- **Pottery and Metalwork:** Pottery was both functional and decorative, with intricate designs and glazes. Metalworkers produced finely crafted tools, weapons, jewelry, and ceremonial objects.

- **Textiles:** Textiles, particularly woolen garments and carpets, were highly valued. Mesopotamian weavers created complex patterns and used natural dyes to produce vibrant colors.

Literature: Mesopotamian literature is among the oldest in the world, with texts inscribed on clay tablets using cuneiform script. Key literary works include:

- **The Epic of Gilgamesh:** This epic poem, one of the earliest known works of literature, tells the story of King Gilgamesh and his quest for immortality. It explores themes of friendship, mortality, and the human condition.

- **Creation Myths:** Mesopotamian creation myths, such as the Enuma Elish, describe the origins of the world and the gods. These texts provide insight into Mesopotamian cosmology and religious beliefs.

- **Hymns and Prayers:** Hymns and prayers to various gods were an important part of religious practice. These texts often praised the gods, sought their favor, and expressed gratitude for their blessings.

Achievements and Contributions

Development of Cuneiform Writing

Origins and Evolution: Cuneiform writing, one of the earliest writing systems, originated in Sumer around 3500 BCE. It began as pictographic symbols used for recordkeeping and gradually evolved into a complex system of wedge-shaped marks impressed on clay tablets. Cuneiform was used for various purposes, including administrative records, legal documents, literature, and scientific texts.

Spread and Influence: The use of cuneiform spread beyond Sumer to other Mesopotamian civilizations, such as Akkad, Babylon, and Assyria. It became a lingua franca of the ancient Near East, used by different cultures for communication and record-keeping. The adaptability of cuneiform allowed it to be used for multiple languages, including Sumerian, Akkadian, Hittite, and Elamite.

Impact on Civilization: The development of cuneiform writing revolutionized communication and administration in ancient Mesopotamia. It facilitated the management of complex societies, enabled the preservation and transmission of knowledge, and laid the foundation for the development of literature, law, and science.

Legal Codes Such as the Code of Hammurabi

The Code of Hammurabi: The Code of Hammurabi, one of the oldest and most comprehensive legal codes, was enacted by King Hammurabi of Babylon around 1754 BCE. Inscribed on a stele and displayed publicly, the code consisted of 282 laws covering various aspects of daily life, including commerce, property, family, and criminal justice.

Principles of Justice: The Code of Hammurabi emphasized the principles of justice and retribution, often summarized by the phrase "an eye for an eye." The code aimed to protect the weak and vulnerable, establish fairness, and maintain social order. It also introduced the concept of presumption of innocence and the right to present evidence in legal disputes.

Influence on Later Legal Systems: The Code of Hammurabi influenced subsequent legal systems in the ancient Near East and beyond. Its principles of justice, legal procedures, and codification of laws served as a model for later civilizations, including the Israelites, Greeks, and Romans. The code's legacy can be seen in modern legal traditions, which continue to uphold the values of justice and fairness.

Innovations in Agriculture, Mathematics, and Astronomy

Agriculture: Mesopotamians made significant advancements in agriculture, developing techniques and tools that increased productivity and supported population growth.

- **Irrigation Systems:** The construction of extensive irrigation networks, including canals, dikes, and reservoirs, allowed for the efficient distribution of water to fields. This innovation enabled the cultivation of crops in areas with limited rainfall and contributed to agricultural surplus.
- **Plowing and Harvesting:** The invention of the plow and improvements in farming tools facilitated soil preparation and crop cultivation. Techniques such as crop rotation and the use of fertilizers enhanced soil fertility and yields.

Mathematics: Mesopotamians made foundational contributions to mathematics, developing concepts and techniques that influenced later civilizations.

- **Numerical System:** The Mesopotamians used a sexagesimal (base-60) numerical system, which facilitated complex calculations and the development of advanced mathematical concepts. This system is the basis for the division of time into hours, minutes, and seconds, as well as the 360- degree circle.
- **Geometry and Measurement:** Mesopotamians applied geometry to land surveying, construction, and astronomy. They developed standardized units of measurement for length, area, and volume, which were essential for trade, engineering, and architecture.

Astronomy: Mesopotamian astronomers made significant observations and developed theories that laid the groundwork for later astronomical studies.

- **Celestial Observations:** Mesopotamian astronomers meticulously recorded the movements of celestial bodies, including the sun, moon, planets, and stars.

Their observations were used to create detailed lunar and solar calendars, predict eclipses, and understand seasonal changes.

- **Astrology and Divination:** Astronomy was closely linked to astrology and divination in Mesopotamian culture. Astronomers interpreted celestial phenomena as omens and used their knowledge to advise rulers and make predictions about the future.

Religion and Mythology

Polytheistic Beliefs and Major Gods

Ancient Mesopotamian religion was polytheistic, with a pantheon of gods and goddesses who controlled various aspects of the natural and human world.

Anu: Anu was the chief god of the Mesopotamian pantheon, associated with the sky and heavens. He was considered the father of the gods and the ruler of the cosmos.

Enlil: Enlil, the god of air and storms, was a powerful and influential deity. He was responsible for the control of the weather, agriculture, and fertility. Enlil's temple in Nippur was a major religious center.

Ishtar (Inanna): Ishtar, also known as Inanna, was the goddess of love, fertility, and war. She was a complex and multifaceted deity, embodying both nurturing and destructive aspects. Ishtar was widely worshipped and had significant influence in Mesopotamian mythology and culture.

Marduk: Marduk, the patron god of Babylon, rose to prominence during the Babylonian Empire. He was associated with creation, order, and justice. The Enuma Elish, a Babylonian creation myth, describes Marduk's victory over chaos and his establishment as the king of the gods.

Other Deities: The Mesopotamian pantheon included numerous other gods and goddesses, each with specific roles and attributes. These deities were worshipped through rituals, offerings, and prayers, and their favor was sought for protection, prosperity, and guidance.

Ziggurats as Religious and Administrative Centers

Structure and Function: Ziggurats were massive stepped pyramids that served as religious and administrative centers in Mesopotamian cities.

Each ziggurat was dedicated to a specific god and housed a temple at its summit. The structure symbolized a bridge between the earth and the divine, allowing priests to perform rituals and communicate with the gods.

Construction: Ziggurats were constructed using mud bricks, with a core of sun-dried bricks and an outer layer of baked bricks. They were often adorned with intricate designs and inscriptions, showcasing the craftsmanship and architectural skills of the Mesopotamians.

Religious Significance: Ziggurats were the focal points of religious life in Mesopotamia. Priests conducted ceremonies, made offerings, and performed sacrifices to honor the gods and seek their blessings. The ziggurat also served as a storage place for sacred objects and a repository for records and archives.

Administrative Role: In addition to their religious functions, ziggurats played a central role in the administration of the city-state. They housed the offices of priests and officials, who managed the economic, legal, and political affairs of the community. The ziggurat complex often included schools, workshops, and granaries, reflecting its multifaceted role in Mesopotamian society.

Mythological Texts Like the Epic of Gilgamesh

The Epic of Gilgamesh: The Epic of Gilgamesh is one of the most significant literary works of ancient Mesopotamia. This epic poem, composed in Akkadian, tells the story of Gilgamesh, the king of Uruk, and his quest for immortality.

- **Plot and Themes:** The epic explores themes of friendship, mortality, heroism, and the human condition. It begins with the exploits of Gilgamesh and his companion Enkidu, their confrontation with the monster Humbaba, and the slaying of the Bull of Heaven. After Enkidu's death, Gilgamesh embarks on a journey to discover the secret of eternal life, ultimately learning that immortality is reserved for the gods and that human beings must accept their mortality.

- **Literary Significance:** The Epic of Gilgamesh is a masterpiece of ancient literature, showcasing the poetic and narrative skills of its creators. It provides valuable insights into Mesopotamian beliefs, values, and worldview, and has influenced later literary and religious traditions.

Other Mythological Texts: Mesopotamian mythology is rich with stories that explain the origins of the world, the roles of the gods, and the nature of human existence.

- **Enuma Elish:** The Enuma Elish is a Babylonian creation myth that describes the battle between the god Marduk and the primordial chaos represented by the goddess Tiamat. The myth explains the creation of the world and the establishment of Marduk as the supreme deity.
- **Descent of Inanna:** This myth recounts the journey of the goddess Inanna (Ishtar) to the underworld and her eventual return. It explores themes of death and rebirth, power, and the cycles of nature.
- **Atrahasis:** The Atrahasis epic tells the story of a great flood sent by the gods to punish humanity for its sins. The hero Atrahasis builds an ark to save himself and his family, paralleling the biblical story of Noah's Ark.

Conclusion

Ancient Mesopotamia, with its fertile lands, innovative achievements, and rich cultural heritage, played a pivotal role in the development of human civilization. Its contributions to writing, law, agriculture, mathematics, and astronomy laid the foundations for future societies and influenced subsequent cultures.

The social structure of Mesopotamia, with its hierarchy of kings, priests, merchants, artisans, and farmers, provided stability and organization to its city-states. Daily life in Mesopotamia was marked by advanced urban planning, diverse economic activities, and vibrant cultural practices.

Mesopotamian religion and mythology, with its pantheon of gods and profound mythological texts, shaped the spiritual and intellectual landscape of the region. The construction of ziggurats and the development of complex religious rituals reflected the deep connection between the Mesopotamians and their deities.

As we explore the legacy of ancient Mesopotamia, we gain a deeper appreciation for its contributions to human history and the enduring influence of its cultural and intellectual achievements. The story of Mesopotamia is a testament to the ingenuity, resilience, and creativity of its people, whose innovations continue to resonate through the ages.

Chapter 8
Ancient China

Ancient China, with its vast history and profound cultural heritage, stands as one of the world's oldest and most influential civilizations. This chapter delves into the geography and early settlements of Ancient China, its societal structures, cultural practices, significant achievements, and the complex tapestry of its religious and mythological beliefs.

Geography and Early Settlement

Location Around the Yellow and Yangtze Rivers

Geographical Significance: Ancient China was centered around two major river systems: the Yellow River (Huang He) and the Yangtze River (Chang Jiang). These rivers played crucial roles in the development of Chinese civilization, providing water for agriculture, facilitating trade, and serving as natural barriers against invasions.

- **The Yellow River:** Often referred to as the "Cradle of Chinese Civilization," the Yellow River's fertile plains supported early agricultural communities. Its frequent flooding deposited rich loess soil, making the surrounding areas highly productive for farming.
- **The Yangtze River:** The Yangtze River, the longest river in Asia, provided a lifeline for the southern regions of Ancient China. Its basin supported diverse agricultural practices, including rice cultivation, which became a staple of the Chinese diet.

Early Settlements: Archaeological evidence indicates that human habitation in China dates back to prehistoric times. Early settlements were primarily agrarian, with communities developing sophisticated farming techniques to manage the river's resources.

- **Banpo Village:** One of the best-preserved Neolithic settlements, Banpo Village, located near the Yellow River, provides insight into early Chinese agricultural and communal life. The site includes well-planned houses, storage pits, and a central meeting hall, indicating a complex social structure.

Early Dynasties: Shang, Zhou, Qin, and Han

The Shang Dynasty (c. 1600-1046 BCE): The Shang Dynasty is recognized as the first historically documented Chinese dynasty, known for its advancements in metallurgy, writing, and urban planning.

- **Capital Cities:** The Shang established several capital cities, including Anyang, where large palaces, temples, and royal tombs have been excavated. These cities served as administrative and religious centers.

- **Bronze Casting:** The Shang are renowned for their bronze casting techniques, producing intricate ritual vessels and weapons. These artifacts highlight the dynasty's technological and artistic achievements.

- **Oracle Bones:** The Shang used oracle bones for divination, inscribing them with questions to the gods. These bones provide the earliest known examples of Chinese writing.

The Zhou Dynasty (c. 1046-256 BCE): The Zhou Dynasty succeeded the Shang and introduced significant cultural and political changes, including the concept of the "Mandate of Heaven."

- **Western Zhou and Eastern Zhou:** The Zhou Dynasty is divided into the Western Zhou and Eastern Zhou periods. The latter includes the Spring and Autumn period and the Warring States period, marked by political fragmentation and philosophical development.

- **Mandate of Heaven:** The Zhou introduced the Mandate of Heaven, a doctrine that justified the ruler's authority as divinely ordained but contingent on virtuous governance. This concept influenced Chinese political thought for millennia.

- **Confucianism and Daoism:** The Zhou period saw the rise of influential philosophies, including Confucianism, founded by Confucius, and Daoism, attributed to Laozi. These philosophies profoundly shaped Chinese society and culture.

The Qin Dynasty (221-206 BCE): The Qin Dynasty, though short-lived, was a pivotal period in Chinese history, marked by the unification of China under a centralized imperial government.

- **Qin Shi Huangdi:** Qin Shi Huangdi, the first emperor of China, implemented sweeping reforms to consolidate power. He standardized weights, measures, and the writing system, and constructed extensive infrastructure, including roads and the Great Wall.

- **Legalism:** The Qin Dynasty embraced Legalism, a philosophy advocating strict laws and harsh punishments to maintain order. Legalist principles underpinned Qin governance and administration.

The Han Dynasty (206 BCE-220 CE): The Han Dynasty followed the Qin and is considered a golden age of Chinese civilization, characterized by political stability, economic prosperity, and cultural flourishing.

- **Liu Bang and the Establishment of the Han:** Liu Bang, a commoner-turned-general, founded the Han Dynasty. His rule and that of his successors strengthened the imperial system and expanded China's borders.

- **Silk Road:** The Han Dynasty facilitated the development of the Silk Road, a network of trade routes connecting China to Central Asia, the Middle East, and Europe. This trade route promoted cultural and economic exchanges.

- **Han Contributions:** The Han Dynasty made significant advancements in technology, science, and culture. Innovations such as paper, the seismograph, and advancements in medicine and astronomy emerged during this period.

Society and Culture

Social Hierarchy: Emperors, Nobles, Scholars, Peasants, Artisans, and Merchants

Ancient Chinese society was organized into a hierarchical structure, with distinct classes based on occupation, wealth, and social status.

Emperors: At the top of the hierarchy was the emperor, regarded as the "Son of Heaven" and the supreme ruler of the empire. The emperor wielded absolute authority and was responsible for maintaining harmony and order within the state.

Nobles: The noble class, including members of the royal family and high-ranking officials, held significant power and influence. Nobles owned large estates, commanded armies, and played key roles in governance and administration.

Scholars: Scholars, often referred to as the literati or gentry, occupied a respected position in society. They were well-educated individuals who passed rigorous civil service examinations to enter government service. Scholars were the backbone of the bureaucratic system, advising the emperor and implementing policies.

Peasants: The majority of the population were peasants who worked the land to produce food. Although they were considered lower in the social hierarchy, peasants were vital to the economy and were often well-regarded for their hard work and contributions to society.

Artisans and Craftsmen: Artisans and craftsmen formed a middle class, skilled in various trades such as pottery, metalworking, weaving, and carpentry. Their work was essential for producing goods and maintaining infrastructure.

Merchants: Merchants engaged in trade and commerce, facilitating the exchange of goods within China and with other regions. Despite their economic importance, merchants were often viewed with suspicion and ranked lower in the social hierarchy due to Confucian ideals that prioritized agriculture and scholarship over commerce.

Daily Life and Cultural Practices

Daily Life: Daily life in ancient China varied widely depending on social status, occupation, and geographic location. However, certain aspects of life were common across different strata of society.

- **Housing:** Housing in ancient China ranged from simple, thatched-roof cottages for peasants to elaborate, multi-story compounds for nobles and wealthy families.

Urban areas featured densely packed homes, while rural areas had more spacious living arrangements.

- **Clothing:** Clothing was an important indicator of social status. Commoners typically wore simple garments made from hemp or cotton, while the elite wore silk robes adorned with intricate embroidery. Clothing styles also varied by region and season.

- **Food and Cuisine:** The Chinese diet was diverse, with staples such as rice, millet, wheat, and vegetables. Meat, fish, and poultry were consumed by those who could afford them. The preparation and consumption of tea became a cultural practice, and communal meals were an important social activity.

Cultural Practices: Ancient Chinese culture was rich and multifaceted, with practices and traditions that have endured for centuries.

- **Festivals and Celebrations:** Festivals such as the Chinese New Year, the Mid-Autumn Festival, and the Dragon Boat Festival were significant cultural events. These celebrations involved rituals, feasts, music, and dance, reflecting the agricultural calendar and religious beliefs.

- **Family and Ancestor Worship:** The family was the fundamental unit of society, with a strong emphasis on filial piety and respect for elders. Ancestor worship was a key aspect of Chinese culture, with rituals performed to honor deceased family members and seek their guidance and protection.

- **Education and Literacy:** Education was highly valued, especially among the elite. The civil service examination system promoted literacy and scholarly achievement, shaping the intellectual and administrative landscape of ancient China.

Contributions to Art, Literature, and Philosophy

Art: Ancient Chinese art is renowned for its diversity and sophistication, encompassing a wide range of media and styles.

- **Calligraphy:** Calligraphy, the art of beautiful writing, was highly esteemed and considered a form of artistic expression. Mastery of calligraphy was a mark of education and cultural refinement.

- **Painting:** Chinese painting, often created on silk or paper, depicted landscapes, flowers, animals, and human figures. Techniques such as ink wash painting emphasized simplicity and harmony with nature.

- **Ceramics:** Chinese pottery and porcelain were highly advanced, with intricate designs and glazes. The development of porcelain during the Tang Dynasty became one of China's most famous artistic achievements.

Literature: Ancient Chinese literature is vast and varied, with genres including poetry, prose, historical texts, and philosophical works.

- **Classical Poetry:** Poetry was a central form of literary expression, with notable poets such as Li Bai and Du Fu producing works that continue to be celebrated. The "Book of Songs" (Shijing) is one of the earliest anthologies of Chinese poetry.

- **Historical Texts:** Historical writing was an important literary tradition. Works like "Records of the Grand Historian" by Sima Qian and the "Book of Han" provided detailed accounts of China's history and set standards for historiography.

- **Philosophical Works:** Philosophical texts, such as Confucius's "Analects," Laozi's "Dao De Jing," and Sun Tzu's "The Art of War," have had profound and lasting impacts on Chinese thought and beyond.

Philosophy: Ancient China was a cradle of philosophical thought, with major schools of philosophy shaping its culture and governance.

- **Confucianism:** Confucianism, founded by Confucius, emphasized moral virtue, social harmony, and the importance of education and familial respect. It became the dominant philosophical system and influenced Chinese society for millennia.

- **Daoism:** Daoism, attributed to Laozi, focused on living in harmony with the Dao (the Way), advocating simplicity, spontaneity, and non-interference with the natural order. It provided a counterbalance to the structured approach of Confucianism.
- **Legalism:** Legalism, developed by thinkers like Han Feizi, emphasized strict laws, central authority, and pragmatic governance. It played a crucial role during the Qin Dynasty's unification of China.
- **Buddhism:** Buddhism, introduced to China from India during the Han Dynasty, offered new perspectives on spirituality, ethics, and the afterlife. It became a major religious and philosophical system, influencing Chinese culture and art.

Achievements and Contributions

Development of Chinese Characters

Origins and Evolution: The Chinese writing system is one of the oldest in the world, with origins tracing back to oracle bone inscriptions of the Shang Dynasty. The characters evolved from pictographs and ideographs into a complex system of logograms.

- **Oracle Bones:** The earliest known Chinese writing is found on oracle bones used for divination during the Shang Dynasty. These inscriptions represent the foundation of Chinese script.
- **Seal Script and Clerical Script:** During the Zhou and Qin dynasties, writing evolved into the seal script and clerical script, which standardized the characters and made them easier to write and read.
- **Standardization:** The Qin Dynasty's unification efforts included standardizing the writing system, which facilitated communication and administration across the vast empire.
- **Calligraphy:** Over time, calligraphy became an esteemed art form, with various styles such as cursive script and regular script. Mastery of calligraphy was a mark of education and cultural refinement.

Impact on Culture: The development of Chinese characters had a profound impact on Chinese culture, enabling the preservation and dissemination of knowledge, literature, and historical records. The writing system played a crucial role in unifying diverse regions and peoples within the Chinese empire.

Philosophies: Confucianism and Daoism

Confucianism: Confucianism, founded by Confucius (Kong Fuzi), emphasized ethics, social harmony, and the importance of education and familial relationships.

- **Key Principles:** Confucianism is based on principles such as "ren" (benevolence), "li" (ritual propriety), "xiao" (filial piety), and "yi" (righteousness). These principles guided personal behavior and social interactions.

- **Influence on Society:** Confucianism became the foundation of Chinese education, governance, and social structure. The civil service examination system, which selected government officials based on their knowledge of Confucian texts, reinforced its influence.

- **Confucius's Legacy:** Confucius's teachings were compiled by his disciples in the "Analects," a collection of sayings and dialogues that became a cornerstone of Chinese literature and philosophy.

Daoism: Daoism, attributed to Laozi, focused on living in harmony with the Dao, the fundamental principle that underlies the natural order of the universe.

- **Key Concepts:** Daoism emphasizes "wu wei" (nonaction or effortless action), "ziran" (naturalness), and "yin-yang" (the interdependence of opposites). These concepts advocate simplicity, spontaneity, and harmony with nature.

- **The Dao De Jing:** The foundational text of Daoism, the "Dao De Jing," attributed to Laozi, consists of poetic verses that explore the nature of the Dao and the art of living in accordance with it.

- **Cultural Influence:** Daoism influenced Chinese art, literature, medicine, and religious practices. It provided a counterbalance to Confucianism, offering a more mystical and individualistic perspective on life.

Technological Innovations: Paper, Gunpowder, the Compass, and Silk Production

Paper: The invention of paper during the Han Dynasty revolutionized communication, education, and recordkeeping.

- **Cai Lun's Contribution:** Cai Lun, a Han court official, is credited with improving the papermaking process around 105 CE. His method used mulberry bark, hemp, and other fibers, producing durable and affordable paper.

- **Impact on Society:** The availability of paper facilitated the spread of literature, government documents, and educational materials. It played a crucial role in the development of Chinese civilization and later spread to other parts of the world.

Gunpowder: The invention of gunpowder in the Tang Dynasty had profound military and technological implications.

- **Alchemy and Discovery:** Chinese alchemists searching for the elixir of immortality accidentally discovered gunpowder. The mixture of saltpeter, sulfur, and charcoal produced explosive properties.

- **Military Applications:** Gunpowder was initially used for fireworks and later adapted for military purposes, including bombs, rockets, and cannons. These innovations transformed warfare and eventually spread to other civilizations.

The Compass: The invention of the magnetic compass during the Han Dynasty revolutionized navigation.

- **Early Compasses:** Early Chinese compasses were made using lodestone, a naturally magnetized mineral, and were used for geomancy and navigation.

- **Maritime Exploration:** The compass enabled more accurate maritime navigation, facilitating trade and exploration. It played a crucial role in the expansion of Chinese influence and interaction with other cultures.

Silk Production: Silk production, known as sericulture, was a highly valued industry in ancient China.

- **Origins and Techniques:** The Chinese mastered the techniques of raising silkworms and processing their cocoons into silk thread. The production of silk fabric became an important economic activity.

- **Silk Road:** Silk was a highly prized commodity, and its trade along the Silk Road connected China with Central Asia, the Middle East, and Europe. The Silk Road facilitated cultural and economic exchanges, enhancing China's influence.

Religion and Mythology

Ancestor Worship and Its Significance

Concept of Ancestor Worship: Ancestor worship was a fundamental aspect of Chinese religious practice, reflecting the deep respect for family and lineage.

- **Ancestral Altars:** Families maintained ancestral altars in their homes, where they offered food, incense, and prayers to deceased relatives. These rituals were believed to ensure the well-being and protection of the family.

- **Tomb Offerings:** During important festivals and occasions, families visited ancestral tombs to make offerings and perform rituals. This practice reinforced family bonds and continuity across generations.

- **Filial Piety:** Ancestor worship was closely linked to the Confucian virtue of filial piety, emphasizing respect and duty towards one's parents and elders. This value permeated all aspects of Chinese society.

Major Gods and Spirits

Pantheon of Deities: Ancient Chinese religion was polytheistic, with a diverse pantheon of gods, spirits, and mythical beings.

- **Shangdi:** Shangdi, or the "Supreme Deity," was considered the highest god, overseeing the universe and human affairs. He was worshipped by the emperor as the mediator between heaven and earth.
- **Tudi Gong:** Tudi Gong, the "Earth God," was a local deity responsible for the land and its fertility. He was worshipped by communities seeking blessings for agriculture and protection from natural disasters.
- **Mazu:** Mazu, the "Goddess of the Sea," was a popular deity among coastal communities. She was believed to protect fishermen and sailors, ensuring safe voyages.
- **Spirits and Ancestors:** In addition to major deities, the Chinese believed in a multitude of spirits, including ancestral spirits, nature spirits, and protective household deities. These spirits played significant roles in daily life and religious practices.

Influence of Buddhism and Other Philosophies

Buddhism: Buddhism was introduced to China from India during the Han Dynasty and became one of the major religions in Chinese history.

- **Spread and Adaptation:** Buddhism spread through trade routes and missionary efforts, adapting to Chinese culture and integrating with existing beliefs. It gained popularity during the Tang Dynasty, when numerous temples and monasteries were established.
- **Buddhist Schools:** Various schools of Buddhism, such as Chan (Zen) and Pure Land, developed unique practices and teachings that resonated with different aspects of Chinese spirituality and philosophy.
- **Art and Literature:** Buddhism influenced Chinese art, literature, and philosophy, inspiring magnificent sculptures, paintings, and literary works. Buddhist texts

were translated into Chinese, contributing to the rich intellectual tradition.

Other Philosophies: In addition to Confucianism, Daoism, and Buddhism, other philosophical and religious traditions influenced ancient Chinese culture.

- **Mohism:** Founded by Mozi, Mohism emphasized universal love, meritocracy, and pragmatic governance. Although it declined in influence, its ethical and social ideas contributed to the philosophical landscape.

- **Legalism:** Legalism, with its focus on law, order, and statecraft, influenced the development of centralized government and legal institutions, particularly during the Qin Dynasty.

Conclusion

Ancient China, with its rich history, diverse cultural practices, and significant contributions to human civilization, stands as a testament to human ingenuity and resilience. Its advancements in writing, philosophy, technology, and art have left an enduring legacy that continues to influence the world today. Understanding ancient China's geography, society, achievements, and religious beliefs provides valuable insights into the foundations of one of the world's oldest and most continuous civilizations.

Chapter 9
Ancient Japan

Ancient Japan, with its unique blend of indigenous culture, borrowed traditions, and geographical isolation, offers a fascinating glimpse into the development of a distinct civilization. This chapter explores the geography and early settlements of Ancient Japan, its societal structures, cultural practices, significant achievements, and the rich tapestry of its religious and mythological beliefs.

Geography and Early Settlement

Location and Early Settlements

Archipelago of Japan:Ancient Japan is situated on an archipelago off the eastern coast of Asia, comprising four main islands: Honshu, Hokkaido, Kyushu, and Shikoku, along with numerous smaller islands. Its location in the Pacific Ring of Fire influenced its geological and cultural development.

Key Regions and Natural Features: Japan's diverse geography, characterized by mountains, forests, rivers, and coastlines, shaped its early settlements and cultural practices.

- **Kanto Plain:** The Kanto Plain on Honshu island, particularly around present-day Tokyo, was one of the earliest and most densely populated regions. Its fertile plains supported agriculture and facilitated trade and communication.

- **Kansai Region:** The Kansai region, centered around Kyoto and Osaka, served as a political and cultural center during various periods of Japanese history. Its strategic location facilitated interactions with neighboring regions and contributed to the spread of ideas and technology.

- **Natural Features:** Japan's natural features, including Mount Fuji, the Japanese Alps, and the Inland Sea, held spiritual significance and influenced artistic representations in literature, poetry, and art.

Early Settlements: Ancient Japan was inhabited by indigenous peoples known as the Jomon and Yayoi, who practiced hunting, fishing, and rudimentary agriculture. The introduction of rice cultivation during the Yayoi period led to the development of settled communities and social complexity.

Society and Culture

Social Structure: Emperors, Nobles, Samurai, Peasants, and Artisans

Ancient Japanese society was organized into a hierarchical structure characterized by distinct social classes and roles.

Emperors: The emperor, believed to be a descendant of the sun goddess Amaterasu, held divine status and served as the ceremonial head of state. While the emperor wielded symbolic authority, political power often rested with other elites.

Nobles: The noble class, comprised of aristocratic families and courtiers, held significant political and administrative influence. They served as advisors to the emperor, governed provinces, and controlled vast estates.

Samurai: The samurai, a warrior class loyal to a feudal lord or daimyo, played a central role in Japanese history. They adhered to a strict code of conduct known as bushido, emphasizing loyalty, honor, and martial prowess.

Peasants: Peasants formed the backbone of Japanese society, comprising the majority of the population. They worked the land as farmers, producing rice, vegetables, and other crops essential for sustenance.

Artisans: Artisans, skilled craftsmen and craftswomen, produced a wide range of goods, including pottery, textiles, weapons, and religious artifacts. Their craftsmanship contributed to Japan's material culture and artistic legacy.

Daily Life and Customs

Rural and Urban Life: Daily life in Ancient Japan varied depending on geographic location, social status, and occupation. Rural communities focused on agriculture, while urban centers like Kyoto and Nara were hubs of political, economic, and cultural activity.

Housing and Architecture: Traditional Japanese architecture, characterized by wooden structures, sliding doors, and tatami mat flooring, reflected harmony with nature and seasonal changes. Homes ranged from simple thatched-roof cottages to elaborate palaces and temples.

Food and Cuisine: The Japanese diet centered around rice, fish, vegetables, and soy products like tofu and miso. Meals were often accompanied by pickled vegetables, seaweed, and seasonal delicacies. Tea, particularly matcha, became integral to Japanese culture and ceremonies.

Clothing and Fashion: Traditional Japanese attire included kimono, obi, and geta, which varied in style, fabric, and decoration based on gender, age, and occasion. Clothing reflected social status and cultural values, with specific colors and motifs associated with different seasons and events.

Arts, Literature, and Festivals

Ancient Japan fostered a rich artistic and literary tradition, characterized by diverse forms of expression and cultural refinement.

Literature: Japanese literature flourished during the Heian period (794-1185), with the emergence of poetic anthologies like the "Manyoshu" and the "Kokinshu." Courtly romances, diaries, and tales such as "The Tale of Genji" showcased the sophistication of Japanese literature.

Visual Arts: Japanese visual arts encompassed a wide range of mediums, including painting, calligraphy, sculpture, and ceramics. Artists drew inspiration from nature, Buddhist themes, and everyday life, producing works of exquisite beauty and craftsmanship.

Performing Arts: Traditional Japanese performing arts, such as Noh theater, kabuki, and bunraku puppetry, captivated audiences with their elaborate costumes, stylized movements, and evocative storytelling.

Festivals and Ceremonies: Festivals played a vital role in Ancient Japanese culture, serving as occasions for religious observance, community bonding, and seasonal celebrations.

- **Shinto Festivals:** Shinto festivals, known as matsuri, honored the kami (spirits or deities) and marked important agricultural and cultural events. These festivals often involved processions, rituals, music, dance, and offerings to the gods.

- **Obon Festival:** The Obon festival, originating from Buddhist traditions, commemorated ancestors and spirits of the deceased. Families cleaned and decorated graves, lit lanterns, and performed folk dances like the bon odori to welcome ancestral spirits.

- **Cherry Blossom Viewing:** Hanami, or cherry blossom viewing, became a cherished springtime tradition. Families and friends gathered in parks and gardens to admire the fleeting beauty of cherry blossoms (sakura) and enjoy picnics under blooming trees.

Achievements and Contributions

Technological and Agricultural Advancements

Rice Cultivation: The cultivation of rice, introduced during the Yayoi period, revolutionized Japanese agriculture and society. Rice became the staple crop, supporting sedentary settlements, population growth, and the emergence of centralized governance.

Irrigation and Terraced Farming: Ancient Japanese farmers developed sophisticated irrigation systems and terraced fields to maximize agricultural productivity in mountainous regions. Techniques such as paddy field cultivation and crop rotation improved soil fertility and water management.

Metalworking and Crafts: Skilled artisans mastered metalworking techniques, producing tools, weapons, and decorative objects from bronze, iron, and later, steel. Craftsmanship extended to ceramics, lacquerware, textiles, and woodworking, exemplified by intricate designs and meticulous attention to detail.

Development of Writing Systems

Oracle Bone Script: Ancient Japanese writing initially borrowed characters from Chinese script, particularly for administrative and ceremonial purposes. Over time, indigenous scripts like kanji and kana emerged, reflecting Japan's linguistic and cultural identity.

Kanji: Kanji, adapted from Chinese characters, served as the primary script for writing Japanese texts, particularly in official documents, literature, and calligraphy. Each kanji character represented a concept or syllable, conveying meaning through visual symbols.

Kana Scripts: Kana scripts, including hiragana and katakana, developed from simplified kanji characters and were phonetic in nature. Hiragana, used for native Japanese words and grammatical endings, facilitated literacy and vernacular writing. Katakana was employed for foreign loanwords and scientific terminology.

Influence on Arts and Architecture

Buddhist Architecture: The introduction of Buddhism to Japan during the Asuka and Nara periods (6th-8th centuries) brought significant architectural innovations. Temples, pagodas, and monastic complexes, influenced by Indian, Chinese, and Korean styles, became centers of religious practice and artistic expression.

Shinto Shrines: Shinto architecture, characterized by simple, wooden structures with distinctive torii gates, reflected reverence for nature and ancestral spirits. Shrines, dedicated to kami, were built in natural settings, embodying the harmonious relationship between humans and the divine.

Zen Gardens and Tea Houses: Zen Buddhism inspired minimalist landscapes and contemplative spaces, such as zen gardens and tea houses. These environments encouraged meditation, reflection, and sensory awareness, fostering spiritual enlightenment and aesthetic appreciation.

Religion and Mythology

Shintoism and Its Beliefs

Nature Worship: Shinto, Japan's indigenous religion, centered on reverence for kami, spirits or deities associated with natural phenomena, ancestors, and sacred places. Shinto rituals and festivals celebrated the cyclical rhythms of nature and sought harmony with the divine.

Shrine Worship: Shinto shrines, or jinja, served as sacred spaces where worshippers offered prayers, purification rituals, and symbolic offerings to the kami. Torii gates marked the boundary between the mundane world and the sacred realm, inviting visitors to enter with reverence.

Ritual Practices: Shinto rituals, performed by priests or shrine maidens (miko), included purification rites, offerings of food and sake, and ceremonial dances (kagura). These rituals sought to maintain balance and harmony in the natural and spiritual realms.

Major Deities and Spirits (Kami)

Amaterasu: Amaterasu, the sun goddess and progenitor of the imperial lineage, held a central position in Shinto mythology. She was revered as the divine ancestress of the Japanese imperial family and the guardian of the nation's prosperity and well-being.

Susanoo: Susanoo, the storm god and brother of Amaterasu, represented the forces of chaos and destruction. Despite his turbulent nature, Susanoo played a role in shaping the natural world and confronting malevolent spirits.

Inari: Inari, the god of rice, fertility, and prosperity, was widely worshipped by farmers, merchants, and samurai. Inari's shrines, adorned with fox statues, attracted devotees seeking blessings for bountiful harvests and business success.

Buddhist Influence and Religious Syncretism

Introduction of Buddhism: Buddhism was introduced to Japan from Korea and China via trade and diplomatic exchanges, gaining royal patronage and influencing religious and cultural practices. Buddhist temples, monasteries, and sacred texts became integral parts of Japanese society.

Syncretic Beliefs: Shinto and Buddhism coexisted harmoniously in Japan, with practitioners adopting syncretic beliefs and rituals that blended indigenous traditions with Buddhist teachings. This syncretism manifested in the worship of Buddhist deities alongside kami and the incorporation of Buddhist iconography in Shinto art and architecture.

Esoteric Buddhism: Esoteric or Tantric Buddhism, introduced during the Heian period, emphasized secret rituals, mantra chanting, and meditation techniques for spiritual enlightenment and protection. Esoteric practices influenced Shingon and Tendai Buddhist sects, fostering mystical experiences and devotion.

Conclusion

Ancient Japan stands as a testament to the resilience, creativity, and spiritual depth of its people. Across millennia, from the Jomon and Yayoi periods to the imperial eras and beyond, Japan's geography, society, culture, and religious beliefs have evolved and flourished, leaving an indelible mark on world history.

The archipelago's rugged terrain, punctuated by mountains, forests, and coastlines, shaped early settlements and cultural practices. From the fertile plains of Honshu to the misty valleys of Kyushu, the land provided sustenance, inspiration, and spiritual sanctuary.

Society in Ancient Japan was characterized by hierarchical structures, with emperors, nobles, samurai, peasants, and artisans each playing vital roles. Daily life revolved around agricultural cycles, communal rituals, and artistic pursuits, fostering a sense of unity and shared identity.

Japan's achievements in technology, agriculture, writing, and the arts reflect the ingenuity and craftsmanship of its people. From the cultivation of rice to the development of kanji and kana scripts, from the construction of Buddhist temples to the refinement of tea ceremonies, Japanese innovations enriched both domestic life and cultural expression.

Religion and mythology were integral to the fabric of Ancient Japanese society, with Shintoism providing a spiritual foundation and Buddhism offering philosophical insights and ethical guidance. Kami and Buddhist deities were revered as guardians and guides, while rituals and festivals celebrated the interconnectedness of humans, nature, and the divine.

As Ancient Japan transitioned through periods of prosperity, conflict, and cultural exchange, its legacy endured, shaping modern Japan, and influencing global culture. From the enduring traditions of cherry blossom viewing to the cutting-edge innovations of contemporary technology, Japan continues to inspire awe and admiration, inviting us to explore the depths of its ancient wisdom and enduring spirit.

Chapter 10
Comparative Analysis

Ancient civilizations, dispersed across the vast expanse of history and geography, exhibit a rich tapestry of shared characteristics and distinctive attributes. This comprehensive comparative analysis endeavors to unravel the complexities of ancient societies, exploring the commonalities that bind them together and the unique features that set them apart. Through an examination of urbanization, writing systems, architectural and technological advancements, governance structures, cultural diversity, and enduring contributions to modern society, we uncover the multifaceted nature of human civilization across time and space.

Common Features of Ancient Civilizations

Urbanization and Complex Societies

One of the defining traits of ancient civilizations was the emergence of urban centers as focal points of political, economic, and cultural life. These cities, teeming with bustling markets, majestic temples, and labyrinthine streets, represented the pinnacle of human achievement in organization and infrastructure. From the majestic pyramids of Egypt to the grand agora of Athens, urbanization heralded a new era of societal complexity, marked by specialization, social stratification, and the division of labor.

Development of Writing and Record-Keeping

The advent of writing systems revolutionized the way ancient civilizations communicated, documented, and preserved their knowledge and heritage. From the earliest cuneiform inscriptions of Mesopotamia to the elegant hieroglyphs of Egypt, writing enabled the recording of historical events, the dissemination of religious teachings, and the codification of legal codes. Scribes, the custodians of literacy, played a pivotal role in administering bureaucratic affairs, maintaining genealogical records, and transcribing literary masterpieces that continue to captivate audiences to this day.

Architectural and Technological Advancements

Ancient civilizations left an indelible mark on the landscape through their architectural achievements and technological innovations. From the towering ziggurats of Sumeria to the awe-inspiring colossi of Rome, these monumental structures stood as testaments to human ingenuity and ambition. Moreover, advancements in metallurgy, irrigation, and transportation revolutionized daily life, enhancing agricultural productivity, facilitating trade networks, and spurring economic development. The legacy of these architectural marvels and technological breakthroughs endures as a testament to the creative genius of ancient civilizations.

Differences and Unique Aspects

Varied Governance Structures

While ancient civilizations shared commonalities in urbanization and technological prowess, they also exhibited diverse governance structures that reflected their unique cultural, political, and historical contexts. Monarchies, such as the pharaonic dynasties of Egypt and the imperial courts of China, centralized power under divine rulers who claimed authority from the heavens. In contrast, the Greek city-states embraced democratic principles, allowing citizens to participate in decisionmaking processes through assemblies and councils. Similarly, the Persian Empire adopted a system of satrapies, granting considerable autonomy to regional governors while maintaining centralized control over key administrative functions.

Cultural and Religious Diversity

Ancient civilizations boasted a rich tapestry of cultural and religious traditions, ranging from polytheistic pantheons to monotheistic faiths and syncretic belief systems. Polytheistic religions, such as those of the Greeks, Romans, and Hindus, worshipped a pantheon of gods and goddesses, each representing different aspects of the natural world and human experience. In contrast, monotheistic faiths like Judaism, Zoroastrianism, and Christianity emphasized the worship of a single deity, fostering ethical monotheism and moral accountability. Moreover, religious syncretism, the blending of indigenous beliefs with foreign influences, gave rise to eclectic traditions that transcended cultural boundaries and enriched the spiritual landscape of ancient civilizations.

Distinct Contributions to Modern Society

The enduring legacy of ancient civilizations reverberates through the corridors of history, shaping the contours of modern society in profound and multifaceted ways. Legal systems, codified in ancient codes such as the Law Code of Hammurabi and the Twelve Tables of Rome, laid the foundation for modern jurisprudence and the rule of law. Philosophical traditions, rooted in the wisdom of ancient thinkers like Confucius, Plato, and Aristotle, continue to inform ethical discourse, political theory, and moral philosophy. Furthermore, cultural heritage, embodied in the art, literature, and architectural marvels of ancient civilizations, serves as a source of inspiration, education, and cultural identity for people around the globe.

Conclusion

In conclusion, the comparative analysis of ancient civilizations offers a panoramic view of human history, illuminating the common threads that bind us together as well as the diverse tapestry of human experience. By exploring the shared features and unique aspects of ancient societies, we gain a deeper appreciation for the complexities of human civilization and the enduring legacy of our ancestors. Moreover, we come to realize that while the civilizations of the past may have faded into the annals of history, their influence continues to reverberate through the corridors of time, shaping the world we inhabit today and inspiring future generations to reach for the stars.

Chapter 11
Conclusion

Ancient civilizations stand as pillars of human history, their legacies intertwined with the fabric of our modern world. From the monumental achievements of Mesopotamia to the philosophical insights of Greece, and the imperial legacy of Rome, the contributions of ancient civilizations reverberate through time, shaping the course of human progress and the foundations of contemporary society. In this concluding chapter, we reflect on the enduring legacy of ancient civilizations, their profound impact on the modern world, and the importance of preserving their historical heritage for future generations.

The Legacy of Ancient Civilizations

The legacy of ancient civilizations is palpable in every aspect of modern life, from governance and law to art, architecture, and philosophy. The innovative spirit of Mesopotamia, with its invention of writing, irrigation, and urban planning, laid the groundwork for modern civilization's reliance on communication, infrastructure, and organized governance. The democratic ideals of Greece, embodied in the principles of citizenship, equality, and civic participation, continue to inspire political movements and institutions around the globe. The engineering marvels of Rome, from its roads and aqueducts to its legal system and republican ideals, serve as enduring symbols of human ingenuity and ambition.

How Ancient Civilizations Have Shaped the Modern World

Ancient civilizations have left an indelible mark on the modern world, shaping its institutions, values, and cultural heritage in profound and multifaceted ways. The concept of democracy, born in the city-states of Greece, remains a guiding principle of governance in countless nations, providing a model for political participation, accountability, and the protection of individual rights. The rule of law, codified in the legal systems of ancient Rome, forms the cornerstone of modern legal systems, ensuring justice, order, and the protection of civil liberties.

Moreover, the artistic and intellectual achievements of ancient civilizations continue to inspire and enrich contemporary culture, from the timeless beauty of Greek sculpture and architecture to the enduring wisdom of philosophical treatises and literary classics. The scientific innovations of ancient civilizations, from the mathematical discoveries of Mesopotamia to the astronomical observations of China, laid the groundwork for modern scientific inquiry and technological advancements, shaping our understanding of the natural world and expanding the frontiers of human knowledge.

The Importance of Preserving Historical Heritage

In an age of rapid globalization and technological advancement, the preservation of historical heritage has never been more vital. Ancient civilizations serve as custodians of humanity's collective memory, reminding us of our shared heritage, values, and aspirations. By preserving archaeological sites, artifacts, and cultural traditions, we honor the contributions of past civilizations and ensure that future generations can learn from their achievements and mistakes.

Moreover, the study of ancient civilizations fosters cross- cultural understanding, empathy, and appreciation for the diversity of human experience. Through archaeological excavations, historical research, and cultural exchange programs, we can bridge the gap between past and present, fostering a deeper appreciation for the richness and complexity of human history.

In conclusion, the legacy of ancient civilizations is a testament to the enduring resilience, creativity, and ingenuity of the human spirit. By studying their achievements, learning from their mistakes, and preserving their historical heritage, we can ensure that the legacy of ancient civilizations continues to inspire and enlighten future generations for centuries to come.

Glossary

Ancient Civilization: A complex society characterized by urban development, social stratification, monumental architecture, writing systems, and significant cultural achievements, typically dating back to prehistoric times.

Cuneiform: One of the earliest known writing systems, developed by the Sumerians in Mesopotamia, consisting of wedge-shaped characters inscribed on clay tablets.

Dynasty: A sequence of rulers from the same family or lineage who govern a particular region or empire, often passing power from one generation to the next.

Hammurabi's Code: A comprehensive set of laws enacted by the Babylonian king Hammurabi around 1754 BCE, inscribed on a stele and considered one of the earliest known legal codes in history.

Hieroglyphics: A system of writing used by ancient Egyptians, consisting of pictorial symbols or glyphs that represent objects, sounds, or ideas.

Indus Valley Civilization: An ancient civilization located in the Indus River valley (modern-day Pakistan and northwest India) known for its well-planned cities, advanced drainage systems, and distinctive pottery, dating back to the Bronze Age.

Polytheism: The belief in or worship of multiple gods or deities, characteristic of many ancient religions such as those of Mesopotamia, Egypt, and Greece.

Satrap: A provincial governor appointed by the Persian king to administer and govern a specific region within the empire.

Shintoism: The indigenous religion of Japan, characterized by the worship of kami (spirits or deities) and reverence for nature, purity, and ritual practices.

Ziggurat: A massive terraced structure built in ancient Mesopotamia, typically associated with religious or administrative purposes, such as temples or administrative centers.

Timeline of Ancient Civilizations

3500 BCE: The rise of the Sumerian civilization in Mesopotamia marks the beginning of recorded history.

3100 BCE: Early Dynastic Period in Egypt; unification of Upper and Lower Egypt under King Narmer.

2600 BCE: Construction of the Great Pyramid of Giza in Egypt.

2000 BCE: The Indus Valley Civilization flourishes in present-day Pakistan and northwest India.

1754 BCE: Hammurabi, king of Babylon, issues his famous code of laws.

1500 BCE: The Mycenaean civilization thrives in ancient Greece; the Shang Dynasty rules in China.

1200 BCE: The collapse of many Bronze Age civilizations, including the Hittites, Mycenaeans, and Minoans.

776 BCE: Traditional date for the first Olympic Games in ancient Greece.

753 BCE: According to legend, the city of Rome is founded.

551 BCE: Birth of Confucius, influential Chinese philosopher.

490 BCE: The Battle of Marathon between Greece and Persia.

431 BCE: Start of the Peloponnesian War between Athens and Sparta.

336 BCE: Alexander the Great becomes king of Macedon.

323 BCE: Death of Alexander the Great; beginning of the Hellenistic period.

221 BCE: Qin Shi Huang becomes the first emperor of a unified China.

146 BCE: Roman conquest of Greece; destruction of Carthage.

31 BCE: Octavian (later Augustus) becomes the first Roman emperor; end of the Roman Republic.

AD 70: Destruction of the Second Temple in Jerusalem by the Romans.

220: End of the Han Dynasty in China; beginning of the Three Kingdoms period.

224: Establishment of the Sassanian Empire in Persia.

313: Edict of Milan grants tolerance to Christianity in the Roman Empire.

476: Traditional date for the fall of the Western Roman Empire.

618: Start of the Tang Dynasty in China; a golden age of Chinese culture.

794: Emperor Kammu moves the capital of Japan to Heian-kyo (modern-day Kyoto).

800: Charlemagne crowned as Holy Roman Emperor by Pope Leo III.

960: Start of the Song Dynasty in China, known for technological advancements.

1066: Norman Conquest of England; Battle of Hastings.

1071: Battle of Manzikert; Seljuk Turks defeat the Byzantine Empire.

1096: Start of the First Crusade.

1215: Signing of the Magna Carta in England, limiting the power of the king.

1271: Marco Polo embarks on his journey to the court of Kublai Khan in China.

1347: Outbreak of the Black Death in Europe.

1453: Fall of Constantinople to the Ottoman Turks; end of the Byzantine Empire.

1492: Christopher Columbus reaches the Americas; beginning of European colonization.

1543: Copernicus publishes his heliocentric theory, challenging the geocentric view of the universe.

1600: Battle of Sekigahara in Japan; beginning of the Tokugawa Shogunate.

1776: Declaration of Independence in the United States; start of the American Revolutionary War.

1789: French Revolution begins with the storming of the Bastille.

Index